1980

Grammar for Teachers

Grammar for Teachers

Perspectives and Definitions

Constance Weaver
Western Michigan University

National Council of Teachers of English
1111 Kenyon Road, Urbana, Illinois 61801

Grateful acknowledgment is made for permission to reprint the following material. Passage from *Teaching Suggestions for 'Sounds Jubilee' and 'Sounds Freedomring'* by Bill Martin, Jr., and Peggy Brown. Copyright © 1975. Reprinted by permission of Holt, Rinehart and Winston, Publishers. "the hours rise up," reprinted from *Tulips & Chimneys*, by E. E. Cummings, with the permission of Liveright Publishing Corporation. Copyright 1923, 1925 and renewed 1951, 1953 by E. E. Cummings. Copyright © 1973, 1976 by Nancy T. Andrews. Copyright © 1973, 1976 by George James Firmage. Illustration from *What Did I Write?* by Marie M. Clay, published by Heinemann Educational Books (N.Z.) Ltd., Auckland. Reprinted by permission of the publisher. Passage from *Communicating: The Heath English Series* by Morton Botel and John Dawkins. Copyright © 1973. Reprinted by permission of D. C. Heath and Company.

Staff Editor: Carol Schanche

Book Design: Tom Kovacs

NCTE Stock Number 18763

© 1979 by the National Council of Teachers of English.
All rights reserved. Printed in the United States of America.

Library of Congress Cataloging in Publication Data

Weaver, Constance.
  Grammar for teachers.

  Bibliography: p.
  1. English language—Study and teaching.   2. English
language—Grammar—Study and teaching.   3. Language arts.
4. Grammar, Comparative and general.   I. National
Council of Teachers of English.   II. Title.
PE1065.W34   428'.007   78-27514
ISBN 0-8141-1876-3

Contents

Preface

This book is intended for preservice and inservice teachers at all levels. It should be especially useful in English education classes, provided it is seen as a foundation rather than as a complete self-teaching text.

The book is in two separable parts. The first part discusses the nature of the language processes and shows some of the ways teachers can put their own knowledge of grammar to use in helping students become better readers and writers. The second part is essentially a grammar handbook, a discussion of the structure of English as approached from three different points of view. Those with little grammar background might prefer to study the grammar handbook first, particularly the section on "Comparing Grammars."

I would like to thank the many people at NCTE who have generously given this project their assistance and support: in particular, the Editorial Board; Carol Schanche, project editor, for her careful editing and attention to detail; and Paul O'Dea, Director of Publications, for his extraordinary patience and helpfulness. I would like also to thank those who collected, prepared, or wrote materials that I have used: Kay Spade and her son Jay; Gregg Jones; Ross Hilden; Sally Varnell; Leslie Hale; and my son John. Also appreciated is the patience and skill of my typists: Linda Fisher, Linda Bell, Lisa LeBlanc, Patsy Bimba, and May Belle Harn. My colleague Michael Clark was kind enough to read and criticize the manuscript, and to him I am very grateful. But my biggest debt of gratitude is owed to my friend and colleague, Theone Hughes, who for years has been both a help and an inspiration. She leads and I follow.

Introduction

For too long, it has simply been assumed that grammar is basic to the English language arts curriculum. Part One of this book explores that assumption, first by looking briefly at summaries of some of the relevant research, next by examining the nature of the language processes, and last by discussing some ways of assessing and assisting the reader and the writer. Part Two of this book describes some of the essentials of English grammar itself, first discussing sentences and parts of sentences as products, next demonstrating some processes of sentence formation, and finally using grammar as a guide to the punctuation of sentences.

The term "grammar" itself is something of a chameleon, taking on different meanings in different contexts. Here are some of those meanings:

1. In its most basic use, "grammar" is more or less synonymous with "sentence structure" and "syntax." In this sense of the term, "grammar" refers to such things as word order, function words, and grammatical endings.

2. In perhaps its most common sense, "grammar" is more or less synonymous with "usage." People talk about "good grammar," meaning the use of socially prestigious grammar. Conversely, there is "bad grammar," the use of grammatical forms and constructions which are not prestigious.

3. In a linguistic sense, a "grammar" of a language is simply a description of the syntactic structure of the language.

4. In a psycholinguistic sense, a "grammar" of a language is a description of the processes by which sentences of the language may be comprehended and produced.

5. In a schoolbook sense, a "grammar" is usually a text for teaching sentence structure (1), usage (2), some particular description of sentence structure (3), some of the processes by which sentences may be comprehended and produced (4), or some combination of these.

Part One is concerned with the first four meanings of the term "grammar," and particularly with the psycholinguistic sense of the term. Part Two exemplifies the fifth meaning of the term because it *is* essentially a schoolbook kind of grammar, though it reflects all the other meanings of "grammar" as well.

1 English Grammar and Teaching

It is no simple matter to determine the appropriate role of grammar in the English language arts curriculum. In order to decide for themselves the value of teaching grammar, teachers need to acquaint themselves not only with results of the relevant research but with the nature of language processes. Accordingly, we will discuss some of the reasons typically offered for the formal teaching of grammar, explore the psycholinguistic nature of language processes, and then turn to the reading and writing processes specifically, with considerable attention to ways of assessing and assisting the reader and the writer. Finally, we will come full circle, back to the question "Of what use is grammar?"

1 The Uses of Grammar

Over the years and the centuries, various reasons have been offered for the teaching of grammar. Among them are these:

1. The study of grammar is important simply because language is a supreme (and perhaps unique) human achievement which deserves to be studied as such.

2. The study of grammar can be an important vehicle for learning to study something as the scientist does.

3. The study of grammar will help people think more clearly, since grammar is a reflection of thought.

4. The study of grammar will help people master a foreign language more readily.

5. The study of grammar will help people master the socially prestigious conventions of spoken and/or written usage.

6. The study of grammar will help people become better users of the language, making them more effective listeners, speakers, readers, and writers.

One can hardly quarrel with the idea that language is intrinsically interesting, except to point out that students are less likely to be interested in the grammar of their language than in various appealing aspects of language *use*, such as the language of advertising, the "double-speak" of government, the language of sexism, and the dialects of various ethnic and cultural groups within our country. Similarly, one can hardly argue with the idea that the study of language *can* help students learn to work like scientists, provided teachers really believe (and are willing to act upon their belief) that the mastery of grammar is less important than helping students discover how to think and how to learn by and for themselves (see Postman and Weingartner 1966).

But what of the other reasons for studying grammar? All of them are based upon the idea that grammar is *useful* in attaining some other goal, with the further implication that studying grammar in isolation from the rest of the curriculum will automatically produce the desired effect.

As long ago as 1950, the *Encyclopedia of Educational Research* summarized the available research (pp. 392-396), concluding that the study of grammar has a negligible effect in helping people think more clearly, and that a knowledge of English grammar does not contribute significantly to achievement in foreign language. Furthermore, the results from tests in grammar, composition, and literary interpretation led to the conclusion that there was little or no relationship between grammar and composition or between grammar and literary interpretation. Further evidence supplementing the early studies indicated that training in formal grammar did not transfer to any significant extent to writing or to recognizing correct English. In general, the experimental evidence revealed a discouraging lack of relationship between grammatical knowledge and the better utilization of expressional skills. Recently grammar has been held to contribute to the better understanding of the sentence. Yet even here, there is discouragingly little relationship between sentence sense and grammatical knowledge of subjects and predicates. On the whole, the more recent research supports the conclusion that the study of grammar in, of, and by itself has little positive effect upon anything else (see, for example, Petrosky 1977). Indeed, even the grammatical knowledge itself is not long retained (*Encyclopedia of Educational Research* 1960).

Why, then, do teachers continue to teach grammar? And why, in fact, is grammar receiving increasingly more attention in many of our schools? Doubtless there are several reasons. One may simply be tradition, the scholarly ideal of preserving our intellectual and cultural heritage or the all too common idea of parents that "what was good enough for us is good enough for our kids." Another reason, certainly, is the pervasive concern for "basic" skills. Our students can't read as well as they should, we are told, and they don't write as well as they ought to, or even as well as students used to (see, for example, the SLATE Starter Sheets, NCTE 1976). In the face of this concern, it is natural to turn to *anything* that might help, including grammar.

Thus teachers are faced with an apparent contradiction. On the one hand, a considerable body of research and the testimony of innumerable students suggest that studying grammar *doesn't* help people read or write better (or, for that matter, listen or speak better either). On the other hand, the public in general and many English and language arts teachers in particular seem convinced that studying grammar *does* help, or at least it should.

One may well wonder what has caused this apparent contradiction. Again, tradition may play a role: the idea that grammar is good for a person has become a hallowed part of our cultural mythology. Another factor may be teachers' firm conviction that *they*, as individuals, have been helped by their study of grammar: that, for example, the study of English grammar has made it easier for them to learn a foreign language; that the study of grammar has helped them improve their sentence structure; or that the study of grammar has helped them learn to use the conventions of written English. It is natural for teachers to assume that if grammar has helped *them*, it should do the same for their students. Unfortunately, this is not commonly the case. This is why, as long ago as 1936, the Curriculum Commission of the National Council of Teachers of English recommended that "all teaching of grammar separate from the manipulation of sentences be discontinued . . . since every scientific attempt to prove that knowledge of grammar is useful has failed . . . " (*Encyclopedia of Educational Research* 1950, p. 392).

That recommendation, while arguing against the teaching of grammar per se, is an incipient rationalization for helping students comprehend grammatical constructions in their reading and manipulate grammatical constructions in their writing. Those who comprehend and use language well are those who have a good *intuitive* grasp of grammar. It would seem logical that poor readers and writers could be helped by a generous dose of grammar, so that they can do consciously what the better readers and writers do unconsciously. However, this is generally not the case. An analogy may help here. It has been found that kindergarteners who know their letter names and sounds at the end of the school year are better first grade readers than those who do not have this knowledge; therefore, it seems logical to teach explicitly the letter names and sounds to kindergarteners. Unfortunately, this approach generally does not have the desired results. Either the children do not learn from direct instruction, or they are not able to put this knowledge into practice in their reading. So it is with grammar: many students simply are unable (or unwilling) to learn the terms and "rules" we try to teach them, and many others are unable (or again, unwilling) to put into practice what they have supposedly learned (see O'Donnell and Smith 1975).

The message seems clear. Students *do* need to develop a good intuitive sense of grammar, but they can do this best through *indirect* rather than direct instruction. Instead of formally teaching them grammar, we need to give them plenty of structured and unstructured opportunities to deal with language directly. If we want them to improve their reading, they must read; if we want them to improve their writing, they must write. This does not mean, of course, that grammar is of no use whatsoever, or that grammatical terminology should be entirely avoided. Rather, it means that teachers need not *teach* grammar so much as use their own knowledge of grammar in helping students understand and use language more effectively.

Language arts teachers and English teachers need, then, not only a knowledge of language structure (grammar), but an understanding of the language processes (listening, speaking, reading, and writing).

2 The Psycholinguistic Nature of the Language Processes

Linguistics is the study of language structure, and psycholinguistics is the study of language processes—listening, speaking, reading, and writing. Language does not exist in a vacuum; we *use* language to think and communicate, to represent, clarify, and express our ideas to ourselves and others. The following survey of the four language processes begins with sentences and the propositions they represent, followed by a more thorough examination of those propositions. Finally, the discussion deals with the acquisition of oracy (listening and speaking) and the acquisition of literacy (reading and writing). Those interested in exploring some of these topics in more depth will find Clark and Clark (1977) an excellent resource.

Sentences and Propositions

Verbal communication involves a *sender* (a speaker or writer), a message, and a *receiver* (a listener or reader, either hypothetical or real). But what is the nature of the message? Obviously, the total message may include far more than what is conveyed by words, because nonverbal communication accompanies what is explicitly said or written.[1] Taking just the verbal part of the message, we might argue intuitively that the basic verbal unit of communication is the sentence, though of course we can talk about smaller and larger units as well. But what is a sentence? Different groups of grammarians and linguists have defined the sentence in different ways (see pp. 102-103). Drawing upon Noam Chomsky's "transformational" model of language, psycholinguists point out that sentences have both a *surface* structure and a *deep* structure. On the one hand, a sentence obviously consists of a linear sequence of clauses, phrases, words, and sounds or letters; this may be termed the surface structure. On the other hand, a sentence clearly has one or more meanings; this may be termed the deep structure. More technically, the deep structure consists of the underlying propositions and the relations among them. When we speak or write, we express propositions in language. When we listen or read, we determine propositions from language. A proposition expresses a state or action and the entities involved in that state or action. Take the sentence *The elephant eats peanuts*. The action is *eats*. The subject of the sentence tells us what entity is being talked about, namely *the elephant*. The direct object tells us the thing being eaten, namely *peanuts*. This set of relationships is shown in propositional notation:

Eat (the elephant, peanuts)

Actually the word *the* reflects an additional underlying proposition, specifying that the elephant is known to both the sender and the receiver of the message; it's not just any old elephant, but the one you and I both know about. Similarly, the word *peanuts* reflects an additional underlying proposition, specifying the number of peanuts as more than one. For present purposes, however, it should be sufficient to say that the sentence *The elephant eats peanuts* reflects the proposition *Eat (the elephant, peanuts)*, plus the appropriate tense and aspect markers indicating that the action is repeated.

Propositions consist of a verbal unit, plus one or more nouns. But as the following examples suggest, the "verbal unit" is sometimes a form of *to be* plus an adjective, a preposition, or even a noun:

Sentence	Verbal unit	Nouns	Proposition
Ebenezer snores.	snores	Ebenezer	Snore (Ebenezer)
John gave peanuts to Ebenezer.	gave	John, peanuts, Ebenezer	Give (John, peanuts, Ebenezer)
Ebenezer is kingly.	is kingly	Ebenezer	Kingly (Ebenezer)
Ebenezer is in the zoo.	is in	Ebenezer, zoo	In (Ebenezer, the zoo)
Ebenezer is king.	is king	Ebenezer	King (Ebenezer).

Ignoring the need for indicators of tense and aspect, consider that the sentences on the left would normally be interpreted as the propositions on the right. Conversely, the propositions on the right may be expressed as the sentences on the left.

Note, however, that there is no one-to-one correlation between surface structure and deep structure, between sentences themselves and the propositions they express. For example:

Sentences	Propositions
John gave peanuts to Ebenezer.	Give (John, peanuts, Ebenezer)
John gave Ebenezer peanuts.	
Visiting relatives can be tiresome.	Tiresome (Visit [relatives, someone])
	Tiresome (Visit [someone, relatives])

In the first example, one proposition has two surface representations (and others are possible, though somewhat awkward). In the second example, one sentence expresses two different underlying propositions. That is, the sentence is ambiguous: either it can be tiresome to have relatives visit, or it can be tiresome to go visit relatives. Or both.

To repeat: there is no one-to-one correspondence between sentences and propositions, between the flow of language and meaning. Consider, again, that a proposition can often be expressed as more than one surface structure, a fact easily illustrated with examples from language acquisition. The two-year-old speaks largely in one-word or two-word "sentences," using intonation, gesture, and other nonverbal means to clarify meaning in a particular context. Thus an utterance like *Eat cookie* may mean "I want a cookie to eat" in one instance and "Daddy is eating my cookie" in another; the child uses a simple surface structure plus other cues to express the underlying proposition(s). Gradually the child becomes able to produce longer and more complex utterances, making the deep structure more and more explicit in the surface of utterances. Let us take, as an example, a child who has been wrongly accused of having eaten a missing cookie. The father, poor suspicious soul, has just accusingly asked his daughter Sally the question "Did you eat the cookie?" (Obviously there must have been only one cookie left or only one cookie in sight, because the father specifies *the* cookie.) The child might merely shake her head from side to side and/or say "No" to express the proposition *False* [*Eat* [*Sally, cookie*]], "It is false that Sally ate the cookie." But what other surface structures might Sally use? If she is about two years old, she may be unable to compose sentences more than two words long. Thus her answer might be "No eat," or "No cookie," uttered with appropriate intonation. (Other alternatives are possible, but less likely.) As the child matures, she will be able to express more and more of the underlying deep structure in the surface structure of her reply. One might predict the following sequence of increasingly mature surface structures:[2]

Utterance	Increasing Complexity
1. *No.* (Obviously this answer is common at any age because, in context, it is adequate to express the underlying proposition.)	1. One morpheme. (The child is able to express just one morpheme per utterance, just one minimal unit of meaning.)
2. *No eat. No cookie.* (The child may produce either utterance or both in sequence,	2. Two morphemes.

with an intonation break between.)

3.	*No ate cookie. Me no ate.*[3] (Either, or both in sequence.)	3.	Three morphemes.
4.	*Me no ate cookie.*	4.	Four morphemes.
5.	*Me no ate the cookie.*	5.	Five morphemes.
6.	*Me didn't ate the cookie.*[4]	6.	Five morphemes. (The form *did* is added to carry the negative.)
7.	*Me didn't eat the cookie.*	7.	Six morphemes. (The tense marker is removed from the main verb, indicating that "past" is now a separate morpheme.)
8.	*I didn't eat the cookie.*[5]	8.	Six morphemes. (The pronoun is now in subject form.)

These details of increasingly complex surface structure may not be entirely correct for any individual child (in particular, the use of *I* is likely to be acquired earlier). Nevertheless, the general pattern of development seems universal. As their linguistic abilities mature, young children seem to go through at least these three overlapping stages in learning to make their utterances conform to adult norms:

1. They express more and more of the nouns or "arguments" that are involved in the proposition. (Step 4 above expresses both *me* and *cookie*.)

2. They express more and more of the grammatical markers, beginning with those that convey meaning. (Step 5 adds the definite article *the*). At the same time, children are learning to combine propositions (Sally might say *Me no ate Daddy cookie* if she thought the cookie had belonged to her father).

3. They make requisite alterations in the surface structure. (Step 6 adds *did* to carry the negative, Step 7 removes the tense marker from the main verb, and Step 8 changes the pronoun from the early all-purpose form *me* to the subject form *I*.)

While there may indeed be some overlap between these stages, it is generally true that the child attends first to deep structure (meaning) and then to surface structure (form).

But why so much attention to learning to speak, when the primary concern here is with reading and writing? There are four major reasons:

1. The language processes all involve propositions. In listening and reading, we extract propositions from the flow of language,

while in speaking and writing we express propositions in language.

2. The language processes all reflect an imperfect correspondence between surface structure and deep structure.

3. The language processes all are active processes. Speaking and writing involve an active expression of propositions in language, while listening and reading involve an active search for propositions.

4. Just as there are natural stages in the child's acquisition of oracy (listening and speaking), so there may be natural stages in the child's acquisition of literacy (reading and writing).

Expressing and Determining Propositions

When we speak and write, we are expressing propositions in language. Consider the following set of propositions:

> Eat (the elephant, peanuts)
> Wrinkled (elephant)
> Old (elephant)

Assuming that "elephant" refers to the same male entity in each of these propositions, there are alternate ways of expressing the propositions, including the following:

> The elephant is wrinkled and old. He eats peanuts.
> The elephant eats peanuts. He is old and wrinkled.
> The wrinkled old elephant eats peanuts.

As speakers and writers, our task is to decide which alternative to choose in expressing a set of propositions. As listeners and readers, our task is to determine propositions from language, in this case to determine that the elephant eats peanuts, that he is wrinkled, and that he is old.

One more example should help illustrate the processes of expressing and determining propositions. Consider the following set of propositions, somewhat simplified for clarity:

> Clean (hydrochloric acid, pipes)   "Hydrochloric acid cleans pipes."
> Harm (hydrochloric acid, pipes)   "Hydrochloric acid harms pipes."
> False (Clean [someone, pipes,   "It is false that one should use
> hydrochloric acid])   hydrochloric acid to clean pipes."

Now suppose you wanted to express these three propositions in one or two sentences. You might say or write, for example: *Hydrochloric acid cleans pipes, but it also harms them; therefore, you should not use hydrochloric acid to clean pipes.* According to Stuart Chase in *The Power of Words*, this is unfortunately *not* the way the U.S. Bureau of Standards chose to reply to a plumber's query about using hydrochloric acid to clean drain pipes. Instead, someone at the Bureau wrote, "The efficacy of hydrochloric acid is indisputable, but the chlorine residue is incompatible with metallic permanence." Unable to extract the underlying propositions, the plumber wrote back. A second letter advised him, "We cannot assume responsibility for the production of toxic and noxious residues with hydrochloric acid, and suggest that you use an alternative procedure." Still baffled, the plumber wrote once more. A final letter ignored the first proposition (that hydrochloric acid does indeed clean pipes) in order to clarify the second one and make its implications (the third proposition) unequivocally clear: "Don't use hydrochloric acid; it eats hell out of the pipes" (*The Power of Words*, p. 259). At last the plumber was able to get the message, to determine the underlying propositions.

This anecdote illustrates what we all know from experience, that communication is fraught with all sorts of difficulties. One is inherent in the structure of language itself, in the fact that surface structure is an inadequate reflection of deep structure. Consider, for example, the following pairs of sentences:

> Dad is barbecuing on the grill.
> Steak is barbecuing on the grill.
>
> The appendectomy was performed by a new surgeon.
> The appendectomy was performed by a new method.

There is nothing in the structure of the first set of sentences to tell us that Dad is doing the barbecuing but the steak is being barbecued, nor is there anything in the second set to tell us that the new surgeon performed the appendectomy but the new method was the means by which it was performed. We immediately know, however, that these are the only sensible interpretations. Clearly, proficient listeners and readers are *active* in their search for the propositions which underlie the flow of language; they bring meaning *to* what they hear and read.[6]

Three observations have been made about the language processes thus far:

1. The language processes all involve propositions.
2. The language processes all involve an imperfect correspondence between surface structure and deep structure.
3. The language processes are all active processes.

The Acquisition of Oracy and Literacy

Finally, there is the fourth and final observation that there may be natural stages in a child's acquisition of literacy, stages that in some ways parallel the stages in a child's acquisition of oracy. Actually this is not so much an observation as a hypothesis, supported by various research studies in progress, and by observations of various sorts. Some of these observations might be stated as follows:

1. Language learners initially attend much more to deep structure (meaning) that to surface structure (form). Specifically, they attend more to the basic elements of underlying propositions than to other words and elements of the sentence.

2. Language learners often make errors that are a sign of progress rather than of regression.

3. Language learners unconsciously formulate hypotheses about the structure of their language and about the nature of the language processes.

The term "language learner" here means the child engaged in mastering any one or more of the language processes. There are doubtless parallels between first-language learning and second-language learning, whether the learner be a child or an adult, but the focus here is on the child mastering these language processes in a first language.

Learning a language is not an all-or-nothing affair: we do not simply learn some underlying language structure and then automatically show equal proficiency in all of the language processes. Certainly there is a common underlying core of linguistic elements, structures, and rules, and there is a common mental storehouse. But it may be that in learning to read and write, the child will tend to recapitulate some of the stages and strategies initially involved in learning to listen and speak.

Consider, first, the observation that language learners initially attend much more to deep structure than to surface structure. This is suggested by children's repetitions of what they have heard, by their own spontaneous utterances, and by their interpretations of what they have heard. Hearing an adult say *Fraser will be unhappy*, a two-year-old might "repeat" the utterance by saying *Fraser unhappy*; asked to repeat *I will read the book*, a two-year-old might say *Read book* (Brown and Bellugi-Klima 1964; Brown and Fraser 1963). In each case the child has reproduced basic elements of the underlying proposition. Such truncated repetitions look remarkably like the utterances that two-year-olds spontaneously produce: *Snoopy bone, Mommy read, Sit chair, Allgone sticky, Big dog, Pick flower, Sweater chair*, and so forth. The child's imitations and the child's spontaneous utterances both preserve only certain basic elements of the underlying propositions. The two-year-old omits most function words and virtually all grammatical endings.

Young children's interpretations of language also show more attention to deep structure than to surface structure. Consider a sentence like *The baby feeds the girl.* A three-year-old will generally take this to mean that the girl feeds the baby, because such an interpretation seems more reasonable. The child ignores the apparent surface structure (agent-action-object) in favor of a deep structure that makes more sense (Strohner and Nelson 1974).

It seems clear, then, that young children attend much more to deep structure than to surface structure, and that they attend particularly to the basic elements of underlying propositions. This is true not only of their early listening and speaking experiences, but also of their early attempts to read and write.

Let us deal with writing first, mainly because there is a growing body of evidence that early writing facilitates reading. One reason may be purely motivational: the child is initially more interested in conveying messages than in receiving messages (a natural consequence of the child's early egocentrism). But another reason is that in the process of sending written messages the child begins to discover, intuitively, some of the principles that govern the printed word (e.g. that a finite number of elements such as letters can be combined in various ways to create a potentially infinite number of words and sentences).

In the prewriting stage, the child may be more concerned with making squiggles and letters than with sending messages (there may be a parallel here with the baby's early babbling). But as the child learns to combine letters to form words, those words tend to be the ones most basic to the underlying propositions the child wants to express.

One illustration of this tendency comes from a classroom activity in which children were given word cards to arrange in order to form comments upon the artwork they had created. Instead of creating sentences which corresponded to their normal speech, they at first tended to concentrate upon the words most basic to their ideas. Many children passed through a four-step process (MacKay, Thompson, and Schaub 1970, as reported in Johnson 1977, p. 298):

1. Set out content words: *my home mum.* This is read by the child as "My mum is at home."
2. Set out content words in order: *my mum home.* "My mum is at home."
3. Set out content words with structure words listed at the end: *mum home my is at.* "My mum is at home."
4. Set out word cards in mature sentence order: *My mum is at home.* "My mum is at home."

Thus these children first emphasized words basic to the underlying propositions they wanted to express.[7]

By the end of the first grade, most children can write messages that are much more detailed and complete. However, it is not unusual for such young writers to omit some of the grammatical endings and/or function words that mark a mature surface structure.[8] Here, for example, the tense markers seem to be missing from all the verbs except *had*, and two function words (*about* and *with*) seem to be missing also:

> One night I had a dream. about a cat the cat Love Me and I dream a Puppy the Puppy Love Me We had Fun We Play ball and We Play Yrne and had dondls of Fun and eat at night and at night We Slape and in the Morning We eat Breakfast and We Play. The End.

Since this child does not leave off grammatical endings in her spoken dialect, there must be some other cause for the missing endings, not to mention the missing prepositions. Teachers and parents have commonly cited carelessness as the cause in such cases, but it may well be instead that such "errors" are the result of a developmental phenomenon: in her concern for expressing the basic elements of her underlying propositions, the child is not able to attend to all the grammatical signals as well. Furthermore, research has demonstrated that in America, at least, the syntactic maturity of children's written sentences does not typically catch up with the syntactic maturity of their spoken sentences until somewhere between the fifth grade and the eighth grade (O'Donnell, Griffin, and Norris 1967; Loban 1976). This suggests that children must to some degree "relearn" surface form as they attempt to express their underlying propositions in written language (see also Shaughnessy's work with college students, 1977).

Beginning readers typically show a similar concentration upon the basic elements of underlying propositions, rather than upon the elements that signal syntactic function. This is shown partly by the kinds of errors that beginning readers make and partly by the simple fact that children learn content words more easily than function words. This fact is ironic, since ten high-frequency function words account for about 25% of all the words in printed matter, and since many function words are taught as early sight words because of their high utility and their typical phonic irregularity. Why, then, should function words be so difficult to learn? Presumably because they are rarely used to express the basic elements of a proposition, and because, out of context, their meaning is so imprecise. The word *at*, for example, has thirty-nine separate meanings listed in the *Oxford English Dictionary*, and so has the word *by*. The words *in* and *with* both have forty meanings listed, and *of* has sixty-nine (Smith 1975, p. 88). The meaning of such function words depends heavily upon context, and many if not most function words are predictable from the content words and their order. It is only logical, then, that beginning readers should attend to words that express the basic elements of underlying propositions more than to other words.

The second observation about the acquisition of the language processes was that language learners often make errors that are a sign of progress rather than of regression. This observation is closely tied to the third, that language learners unconsciously formulate hypotheses about the structure of their language and about the nature of the language processes. Both observations are difficult to illustrate with listening, but easy to demonstrate with speech. In the early stages of learning a language, children seem to learn many of the common "irregular" past tense verb forms by rote, apparently without realizing that these contain two separable concepts, the concept of the basic verb (*eat, go, buy,* etc.) and the concept of pastness (as in *ate, went, bought*). Then, having heard many regular past tense forms (*walked, played, waited*), the child seems to formulate an unconscious hypothesis: that to make verbs show past time, you add an *-ed* (pronounced as /t/, /d/, or /ɪd/, depending on what sound precedes). This new hypothesis leads the child to produce not only "correct" past tense forms like *walked, played,* and *waited,* but also some "incorrect" forms like *eated, goed,* and *buyed* (and possibly some "double pasts" like *ated, wented,* and *boughted*). In other words, the child overapplies the rule, and must next learn the exceptions. But the errors themselves must be considered signs of progress because they show that the child has begun to recognize an important rule of the English language. Much the same thing happens with other rules, such as plurals, so that for a while the child is likely to say *tooths* and *mouses, mens* and *childrens.*

The development of yes/no questions, WH-word questions, and negatives provides another interesting example of how errors and progress are intertwined. Let us assume that positive statements are somehow basic to the language, and that questions and negatives are created from an underlying positive statement form. As children's language abilities mature, there seems to be an increasing limit to the number of operations the child can perform upon the basic underlying form. For an illustration, let us take *He can do it* as representing a basic form. The child's increasing production limits might be illustrated as follows (see Belugi-Klima 1971, pp. 100-101):

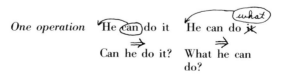

One operation   He can do it   He can do it (what)
                  ⇒   ⇒
                  Can he do it?   What he can
                                  do?

Two operations

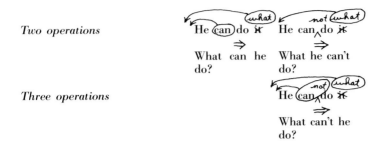

Three operations

One could quibble, of course, over the precise number of operations involved. But the point is that as children try to create increasingly complex sentences (complex semantically and/or syntactically), they will make errors. Many of these errors will be predictable and systematic, like the errors exemplified above in *What he can do?* and in *What he can't do?* Some will doubtless be unpredictable. But such errors, such apparent regressions and inconsistencies, are a natural part of language learning.

Marie Clay (1975) shows that as young writers attempt new challenges, they often exhibit new errors in letter formation and spacing. Also, the pattern of their spelling errors changes as they learn and initially overapply new rules. For example, a child who first spelled *meat* as "met" might spell the word "mete" once he or she has learned about the silent *e* (see Beers and Henderson 1977).

Less seems to be known about the kinds of grammatical errors children make as they gain increasing mastery over the writing process, probably because such errors have often been dismissed as simply mistakes, the results of carelessness. However, at least some of these "mistakes" are positive evidence that the child is trying to express an increasing number of propositions and/or is trying to combine these propositions in increasingly complex ways. A beginning writer who has previously produced papers with only one or two short, "correct" sentences may suddenly begin to write more sentences, but with some errors in grammar—provided the teacher doesn't squelch these efforts by insisting on absolute correctness. Such may be the case with the child who wrote a relatively long description of her dream about a puppy, a description from which she omitted the verb endings and two prepositions. When children try to combine their propositions in increasingly complex ways, they may get lost in their own sentence structure. Such seems to have been the case with the young child who wrote "The boy who had some wings to fly like the birds" (Clay 1975, p. 17).

Similar things happen with both younger and older children as they try to combine propositions in more complex and sophisticated ways. Such writers hypothesize that their underlying propositions can be expressed either in a comfortable, relatively simple structure or in a "new," more complicated structure. The writer opts for the more complicated construction, but makes an error in its execution. Such errors are often relatively superficial, as with the following errors in punctuation:

> He knew he could win. Because he was in top condition.
> He lost his watch. Which he had just bought last week.

In both of these cases, the writers could have simply juxtaposed the underlying propositions:

> He knew he could win. He was in top condition.
> He lost his watch. He had just bought it last week.

Instead of juxtaposing, they chose to subordinate. And as students first begin to subordinate one clause to another, they tend to make the major changes but may ignore the relatively minor matter of punctuation (McCaig 1977b). Again, perhaps there is a limit on the number of processes to which they can attend. At any rate, it is clear that errors do not simply disappear as the child becomes more proficient in writing. Increased syntactic maturity simply brings about different kinds of errors (Mellon 1975). Thus with writing as with speaking, error and progress often go hand in hand.

With reading, the picture is similar. A changing pattern of errors can indeed mean progress: with reading as well as with writing, an increase in proficiency causes different, more sophisticated kinds of errors, errors which reflect an increased ability to glean the meaning of the text (Y. Goodman 1976). More generally, however, reading errors indicate the kinds of strategies the reader is using in processing the written language. One such strategy is the continual formation of hypotheses about the text, since the good reader is one who predicts, a matter dealt with in the next section. Here, however, the concern is with the question of whether hypothesis formation plays a global role in the acquisition of reading ability. One possibility is that the child goes through a series of stages, each reflecting a different hypothesis as to what reading is all about.

Consider the child who has often been read to. This child, at least, tends to come to reading instruction with a hypothesis that might be expressed as follows:

1. Reading means getting meaning from printed material (that is, reading means getting the underlying meaning, the deep structure).

In the conviction that meaning is all-important, such a beginner will even "read" memorized stories, with little regard for the actual words on the page. When the child's free renditions become somewhat more constrained by the teacher and the text, the child may still make major changes in the surface structure of the text as he or she tries to render the deep structure. The following illustration is from a first grader in his second month of reading instruction. The words in italics indicate the child's departures from the text, with the child's successive renditions numbered 1 and 2 respectively:

> 2. *The ball is stuck.*
> 1. *I want the ball.*
> Mike said, "The ball! The ball!"   [The picture shows Mike reaching unsuccessfully toward the ball, which is caught in a tree.]

Here, the child has used verbal and pictorial context to preserve the deep structure, the essential meaning of the text.

As a result of instruction, the child may come to adopt a different hypothesis about reading:

2. Reading means identifying the words (that is, reading means getting the form, the surface structure).

As a result of this hypothesis, the child may begin to exhibit partially different reading habits than before. A child who would originally have used context to render the printed word *canary* as "bird," for example, may now struggle to sound out the specific word *canary*. If the child has not totally abandoned the hypothesis that reading means getting meaning, he or she may combine the search for meaning with the use of phonics to come up with the concept of bird but a nonword like "cainery"; here the error can be construed as a sign of progress. Similarly, a child who is familiar with canaries may combine the search for meaning with a minimal use of phonics to come up with the concept *and* the actual word "canary." In short, the child may quickly learn to combine the first two hypotheses about reading to produce a third:

3. Reading means identifying as many of the words as necessary in order to get meaning (that is, reading means using surface structure as a means for determining deep structure).

This seems to be one of the basic hypotheses of effective and efficient readers, whether they be age five or fifty.

Note, however, that this series of stages is not necessarily a "natural" one, parallel to the stages we have discussed in speaking and writing acquisition. Rather, these stages may be very much dependent upon the child's environment and instruction.

Consider now the child who has seldom been read to, either in the home or at school. Such a child may never have formulated hypothesis 1 before formulating hypothesis 2, that reading means identifying words. If the child doesn't expect reading to make sense, he or she may deal with each word as if it stood in isolation—and that in turn makes the task of word identification much more difficult. In one study, for example, Ken Goodman had children read words first in isolation and then in the context of a story (1965, p. 640). In context, his first grade group correctly read 62% of the words that they had missed in isolation, his second graders correctly read 75% of the words they had missed in isolation, and his third graders correctly read 82% of the words they had missed in isolation. Even adults can recognize words more readily and more accurately in context than in isolation, so the child who treats each word as if it were part of a word list is obviously at a disadvantage. Unfortunately, all too many children never seem to progress beyond this stage. This is particularly likely to happen if (1) the child has seldom been read to, and/or (2) the child's reading instruction has directly or indirectly encouraged the child to focus upon words as if they existed in isolation. Such a child may be slow to formulate the hypothesis of proficient readers, that reading means identifying as many of the words as necessary in order to get meaning.

Returning to writing, we might postulate a similar series of stages, though again these stages may be more instruction-imposed than developmental. A beginning writer's initial hypothesis about writing might go something like this:[9]

1. Writing means expressing meaning in written language (that is, writing means expressing deep structure).

Failure to communicate and/or instructional emphasis on "correctness" may result in a second hypothesis:

2. Writing means producing sequences of words with correct usage, sentence structure, punctuation, capitalization, and spelling (that is, writing means producing a "correct" surface structure).

The fortunate student will either bypass this stage completely or progress to a third, as represented by hypothesis 3:

3. Writing means using as many conventions of usage, sentence structure, punctuation, capitalization, and spelling as necessary to convey meaning (that is, writing means using surface structure to *convey* deep structure).

Such a hypothesis may be narrow or broad, depending on the degree to which the writer takes account of the reader's expectations about surface "correctness." As with reading, however, there is danger that the child may be slow to relinquish a hypothesis such as the second. This is particularly true if, time and again, teachers respond to the child's writing mainly by commenting on various aspects of mechanics. Unfortunately, such children may never develop anything like hypothesis 3.

Summary

There are not only commonalities among the language processes themselves but commonalities in the way that children acquire the use of the language processes. The language processes all involve propositions. All reflect an imperfect relationship between surface structure and deep structure, and all are active processes. Just as there are natural stages in the child's acquisition of oracy, so there may be natural stages (and/or instruction-induced stages) in a child's acquisition of literacy. This hypothesis rests upon various observations, including the observations that language learners (1) initially are concerned much more with deep structure than with surface structure, (2) often make errors that are a sign of progress rather than of regression, and (3) unconsciously formulate hypotheses about the structure of their language and about the nature of the language processes. Some of the instructional implications should become increasingly clear in the sections that follow.

3 Grammar and Reading

Previous discussion has emphasized the fact that listening and reading involve determining underlying propositions and their relationships, the fact that surface grammar does not always signal the relationships between words, and the fact that listening and reading involve an *active* search for meaning. In order to help teachers decide how grammar should fit into the reading program, these points should be developed, with particular focus on the reading process. More about the reading process can be learned from Cooper and Petrosky (1976), Smith (1973), Smith (1975), Smith (1978), and Carton (1976).

The Reading Process

Listening and reading are active processes. What does this mean? Among other things, it means that as we listen and read we are constantly forming hypotheses, forming predictions about what will come next. Consider, for example, the responses from a six-year-old when asked how one might complete the sentence "Mommy fell in the _____." He offered the following possibilities: *well, pond, tub, big ocean, whale's tummy.* The remarkable thing about these responses is that they are not remarkable, at least not syntactically; they are all nouns or noun phrases (adjective + noun combinations), precisely what one would expect after the determiner *the.* The responses fit semantically, too; Mommy could conceivably fall into any one of these things, though some are more likely than others.

Less obvious, perhaps, is the fact that we use even *following* context to interpret the words that we hear and read. In one experiment, people were presented with one of the following tape-recorded sentences. (The asterisk represents a cough.)

> It was found that the *eel was on the axle.
> It was found that the *eel was on the shoe.
> It was found that the *eel was on the orange.
> It was found that the *eel was on the table.

The only difference among the four sentences was the word spliced onto

22

the end of the sentence (*axle, shoe, orange, table*). Depending on which version people listened to, *eel was "heard" as *wheel, heel, peel,* and *meal* respectively (Warren and Warren 1970). That is, *eel was interpreted in accordance with the meaning of something that occurred four words later in the sentence. Much the same thing occurs in normal listening and reading. To test this for yourself, you might try reading the following sentences aloud quickly, without prereading them silently:

> The bass doesn't sound right.
> There were some tears in her eyes.
> She stared at the minute hand on the clock.
> I don't like the lead singer.

Chances are that you pronounced *bass* to rhyme with *base, tears* to rhyme with *cheers, minute* to rhyme with *linnet,* and *lead* to rhyme with *greed.* In some cases sheer semantic probability may have suggested the right interpretation, but the only way of knowing the pronunciation for certain was to look farther ahead in the sentence. Research shows that this is in fact what we normally do in reading: our eyes are normally about four words ahead of the word we are focusing on, and we use this following context to aid us in word identification (Levin and Kaplan 1970).

In listening and reading, then, we normally use four kinds of context: syntactic and semantic both preceding and following the word in question. We use preceding grammar and meaning to predict (formulate hypotheses about) what is coming next, and we use following grammar and meaning to confirm and/or correct those predictions.

The best way to determine whether a reader is making use of preceding and following grammar and of preceding and following meaning is to examine *in context* the reader's miscues, the ways in which the reader departs from the text in reading aloud. But *how* do readers go about using context, *how* do they formulate, test and confirm or correct hypotheses, *how* do they determine the propositions that underlie the flow of language? We have two major hypotheses as partial explanations for how we process incoming language.

Syntactic Hypothesis

The syntactic hypothesis is the idea that we use surface structure grammar to group words into syntactic units called *constituents.* That is, we intuitively use function words and other syntactic signals to group words into constituents called noun phrases, prepositional phrases, subject phrases, verb phrases, predicate phrases, and clauses. For example, it seems plausible to assume that we might use some such strategy as the following (Kimball 1973, as adapted in Clark and Clark 1977, pp. 59-61):

> Whenever you find a function word, begin a new constituent larger than one word, and look for content words appropriate to that type of constituent.

More specifically, we might use the following substrategies (adapted from Clark and Clark 1977, pp. 59 and 62):

Strategy a: Noun phrases

Whenever you find an article (*a, an, the*) or quantifier (*some, all, many, two, six,* etc.), begin a new noun phrase. Look for a noun which closes out the noun phrase (as in *the dirty old man*).

Strategy b: Prepositional phrases

Whenever you find a preposition (*to, at, in,* etc.), begin a new prepositional phrase. Look for a noun phrase which closes out the prepositional phrase (as in *through the broken window*).

Strategy c: Verb phrases

Whenever you find an auxiliary verb with tense (*is, are, was, were, have, can, could,* etc.), begin a new verb phrase. Look for a main verb, which ordinarily closes out the verb phrase (as in *would have been going*).

Strategy d: Relative clauses

Whenever you find a relative pronoun (*that, which, who, whom*), begin a new clause. Look for a relative clause, which is in effect a sentence with one noun phrase replaced by the relative pronoun (as in *the man that I saw*).

Strategy e: Adverbial clauses

Whenever you find a subordinating conjunction (*because, when, since, if,* etc.), begin a new clause. Look for a sentence following the subordinator (as in *although he was drunk*).

Strategy f: Nominal clauses and near-clauses

Whenever you find a complementizer (*that, for-to,* etc.), look for a full or reduced sentence (as in *Mary knew that I left,* and *I'd like for you to leave*).

Strategy g: Coordinate constructions

Whenever you find a coordinating conjunction (*and, but, for, nor, or, so*) begin a new constituent similar to the one you just completed. Look for content words of the same kind identified in the previous constituent (as in *Mary and Bill*).

Although we are not usually conscious of using such strategies, they seem intuitively plausible. Strategy a, for example, was exhibited by the six-year-old completing the sentence "Mommy fell in the _____." And the other six strategies also seem plausible, if not quite as simple. Furthermore, such strategies would certainly aid in determining underlying propositions. After isolating the noun phrase *the dirty old man*, for example, we can readily extract the propositions *Old (man)* and *Dirty (man)*.

You can demonstrate your own intuitive use of grammar (function words, grammatical endings, and word order) by reading the following nonsense passage and answering the subsequent "comprehension" questions.

> Corandic is an emurient grof with many fribs; it granks from corite, an olg which cargs like lange. Corite grinkles several other tarances, which garkers excarp by glarcking the corite and starping it in tranker-clarped storbs. The tarances starp a chark which is exparged with worters, branking a slorp. This slorp is garped through several other corusces, finally frasting a pragety, blickant crankle: coranda. Coranda is a cargurt, grinkling corandic and borigen. The corandic is nacerated from the borigen by means of loracity. Thus garkers finally thrap a glick, bracht, glupous grapant, corandic, which granks in many starps.
>
> 1. What is corandic?
> 2. What does corandic grank from?
> 3. How do garkers excarp the tarances from the corite?
> 4. What does the slorp finally frast?
> 5. What is coranda?
> 6. How is the corandic nacerated from the borigen?
> 7. What do the garkers finally thrap?

One doesn't need an understanding of the "topic" to answer such questions, or even to determine the underlying propositions: underlying the relative clause *which garkers excarp*, for example, is the proposition *Excarp (garkers, tarances)*. Simple. All one needs is a good intuitive grasp of grammar, an awareness of syntactic constituents or "chunks."

Even beginning readers make use of such intuitive knowledge, if they are operating on the hypothesis that reading means getting meaning: after all, that is what grammar is *for*, to convey certain kinds of relational meanings. Weber's research with first graders provided ample evidence of this fact when she studied the children's miscues (a miscue is simply any departure from the text). Specifically, Weber examined children's substitution miscues to see what percentage were grammatically acceptable with the prior context only, and what percentage were grammatically acceptable with the following context as well:

Grammatical with preceding context only:	*and* Spot can help Dick.
Grammatical with both preceding and following context:	*hear* Spot can help Dick.

In the first example, the miscue *and* is not grammatical with the following context; in the second example, however, the miscue *hear* fits with both preceding grammar and following grammar. Weber found that about 90% of her first graders' miscues were grammatically acceptable with what preceded them in the sentence, while over 60% of the miscues were grammatically acceptable with the following context as well (Weber 1970, pp. 153 and 160).

But it is not only substitution miscues that preserve grammatical acceptability. Consider this set of miscues from a reader with about two months of reading instruction:

Substitutions

Get a ball, Mary *the*

Who rides with Mike?

Mary rides with Mike. *can ride*

Insertion

Mary said, "Play ball, Jeff.

Mike and I want to play." *ball*

Reversal and insertion

Mike said, "I can't ride.

I can't play with Jeff and Mary. *Mary and Jeff*

I can play ball." *but*

Omission

Velvet will go (on) up the tree.

In each case the miscue results in a grammatically correct sentence, and in some cases the miscue makes the meaning even more explicit than in the original.

Given the various kinds of evidence, then, it seems indisputable that we use our intuitive knowledge of grammar and various kinds of syntactic strategies to chunk the flow of language into syntactic constituents. But it also seems indisputable that these kinds of strategies cannot entirely account for how we determine the underlying propositions and their relations as we process the flow of language.

Semantic Hypothesis

In addition to the syntactic hypothesis we need a *semantic* hypothesis, reflecting the facts that (1) we bring meaning *to* what we hear and read and (2) we determine grammar to a large extent from meaning. It has been suggested, for example, that listeners and readers adopt a general semantic strategy such as this (see Clark and Clark 1977, p. 73 ff.):

> Using content words alone, build propositions that make sense and
> parse the sentence into constituents accordingly.

This reflects the semantic hypothesis in perhaps its strongest form.

Since it is often asserted that we need to know the grammar of a
sentence in order to get its meaning, it may at first seem ridiculous to
assert that we do (or even can) determine grammar from meaning.
However, various kinds of evidence suggest that we do precisely this.
Take this sentence:

> Marge was seated by the usher.

Out of context, this sentence could mean either that Marge was sitting
next to the usher, or that the usher showed Marge to her seat. Until we
know what the sentence *means*, we cannot tell whether it is grammatically active or passive. If the usher showed Marge to her seat, then
"usher" is the agent, the doer of the action, and the sentence is
grammatically passive. But if Marge was sitting next to the usher,
"usher" indicates the location, and the sentence is grammatically active.
We must use meaning to determine the underlying grammatical structure of the sentence.

Pollack and Pickett (1964) surreptitiously recorded some people in
spontaneous conversation, then excised single words from the tape
recordings and played these single words to other people for identification. Single words removed from the normal stream of speech were
correctly identified only 47% of the time. The investigators did not
distinguish between function words and content words in this experiment, but they did compare short monosyllabic words with longer
bisyllabic words; apparently the shorter words were nearly impossible to
identify in isolation. Since many of our most common function words
are extremely short (*a*, *the*, *and*, *but*, *in*, *on*, and so forth), this
experiment suggests that function words would not be much help in
interpreting normal speech. Indeed, it seems likely that we often use
context, content words, and word order to determine which function
words we have heard. We have the impression that we hear most of what
a speaker says, but in fact what we "hear" is to a considerable extent a
construct of the mind, an attempt to make sense out of only partial
auditory input.

Evidence for such a statement is provided not only by laboratory
experiments but by our all too common habit of misinterpreting
people's actual words because of our expectations and preconceptions.
Inquiring about the group attending my conference session on Black
English, someone once asked me, "How white is the audience?" What I
"heard" was "How wide is the audience?" I was more conscious of the

diversity in academic background than of the narrowness in ethnic background.

Recalling such examples from our own day-to-day interactions with family and friends, we may be willing to concede the point that we actually hear less than we think we hear, that in our active search for meaning we are able to fill in many of the unintelligible or missing pieces, particularly the function words. But what about reading? After all, the words are right there on the page for us to see! However, it is often not necessary for us to see the function words, the words that supposedly signal many of the underlying relationships.

To determine this for yourself, try to supply the function words that are missing from the following passage from the *New York Times*, May 5, 1970:[10]

People usually find that in each case they can supply a reasonable function word, often the precise one that was omitted from the original. Studies have shown that we can identify words from only a fraction of the visual information available to us. It appears, too, that we can interpret *sentences* from far less than the total number of words normally available to us. Just as we can usually determine the underlying propositions from children's two-word utterances and the overall context, so we can usually determine the underlying propositions from the content words, word order, and the overall context of what we are reading. In both cases, we can then supply the missing grammatical elements.

Perhaps the most convincing evidence of this comes from normal reading itself, as revealed by reading miscues. A considerable body of evidence indicates that miscues involving function words are fairly common with many *good* readers, those who get the meaning of what they read (see, for example, Y. Goodman 1976). The following are some examples (Goodman and Burke 1973, pp. 166-177):

Substitutions	*might* "You may be right."
Insertions	*up* It was enough to wake ∧ the dead.
Omissions	... as she edged farther into the hollow so (that) the coyotes could not get behind her.
Transformations	*for me to do is* "I think the best thing to do is for me to ... "

All of these miscues result in grammatical sentences, and all of them preserve the underlying meaning. The fact that good readers make far fewer miscues on content words than on function words suggests that they use the content words and word order to determine the underlying propositions and their relations, then produce a surface structure which may be in part their own rather than the author's. They assume that reading means not only using surface structure as a means for determining deep structure, but also using deep structure as a means for determining surface structure.

Certainly there is considerable evidence that we go from surface structure to meaning and then to oral surface structure as we read aloud. Part of this evidence is indirect, from studies of oral repetition and manual copying. One interesting study involved a child who at the time was two years and four months old. She was asked to imitate (repeat) some sentences which contained a relative clause modifying the subject (a construction that tends to be awkward, even for adults). The chart below shows the adult model and Echo's imitations (Slobin and Welsh 1973, pp. 493-494). "Mozart" was the name of the child's bear:

Adult model	*Child's imitation*
Mozart who cried came to my party	⇒ Mozart cried and he came to my party
The owl who eats candy runs fast	⇒ Owl eat a candy and he run fast
The man who I saw yesterday got wet	⇒ I saw the man and he got wet
The man who I saw yesterday runs fast	⇒ I saw the man and he run fast

Remarkably, the child was able to extract the essence of the underlying propositions. But in "imitating" the sentences, she translated the deep structure into her own, less sophisticated surface structure: one independent clause followed by another, rather than a relative clause embedded within an independent clause.

Figure 1. Six-year-old's copying of words.

Another interesting example comes from my son's "copying" of words that his father had written for him, and that the child had read (see figure 1). In several cases the adult's lower-case letter became an upper-case letter in the child's version. That is, he went from the surface structure of the original (e.g. the lower-case *a*, *e*, *h*) to the underlying deep structure (the *concept* of "a," "e," "h"). He then embodied that concept in his own surface structure, the upper-case letter. This example indicates why even respectable scholars are prone to make "mistakes" in copying a passage they want to quote!

So it is with reading. Reading involves an ongoing interaction between the mind of the reader and the language of the text. In general, when reading aloud (or when subvocalizing), the proficient reader goes from surface structure to deep structure and *then* back to surface structure, as suggested by the previous examples of reading miscues. Most of these examples were from first and second graders, suggesting that even beginning readers may encode the meaning of the text into their own surface structure. Of course, sometimes a reader is not trying to get meaning, but only trying to produce an acceptable surface structure. Even then, however, the reader may be forced to go to deep structure in order to produce an acceptable sentence. Consider, for example, the following set of sentences, some of which we have already discussed:

> There were some tears in her eyes.
> Copper pipes are better than lead.
> The bass doesn't sound right.
> He mended the tear in his pants.
> I don't like the lead singer.
> The bass aren't biting today.

Most people can read this list with little if any stumbling, even though they must use meaning in order to pronounce *tears*, *lead*, and *bass* correctly. This again reinforces the idea that reading is an active process of determining underlying propositions and their relationships, and that readers do in fact determine underlying propositions and their relations before producing surface structure.

Dialect-based miscues offer an interesting confirmation of these facts. A college student once made the following kind of miscue in reading aloud part of a paper she had written:

> *if we could go*
> We asked could we go ...

This is an unusual example in that the student's oral rendition used "standard" grammar while her written version used what some would consider a nonstandard construction. Actually, the same thing happened with second and third graders who had learned to read from texts written in standard grammar but were then asked to read stories written in an approximation of Black English grammar, the kind of grammar they themselves used in speech. Just like the college student, they often translated the "nonstandard" grammar of the text into the standard grammar that they were used to seeing in print. Having understood the deep structure, they expressed it in a slightly altered surface structure (Simons and Johnson 1974).

Of course the more usual situation is that children who speak a "nonstandard" dialect will produce some features of that dialect in reading aloud, instead of producing all of the surface grammatical features signaled by the text itself. *We were going* may be read as "We was going," or *I don't have any* may be read as "I don't have none." Such translations, however, are much less frequent than the omission of inflectional endings that are not a systematic part of the reader's dialect. Goodman and his associates have found, for example, that among inner city black children, the following are the most common dialect-related miscues involving grammar (adapted from K. Goodman and C. Buck 1973, p. 9):

1. Absence of past tense marker:
   look for *looked, call* for *called, wreck* for *wrecked, love* for *loved, pound* for *pounded, help* for *helped, use* for *used, run* for *ran, have* for *had, keep* for *kept, do* for *did*

2. Absence of plural noun marker:
   thing for *things, work* for *works, story* for *stories, prize* for *prizes*

3. Absence of third person singular verb marker:
   look for *looks, work* for *works, hide* for *hides*

4. Absence of possessive noun marker:
   Freddie for *Freddie's, Mr. Vine* for *Mr. Vine's, one* for *one's, it* for *its*

5. Substitution and omission of forms of *to be*:
   was for *were, is* for *are, we* for *we're, he be talking* for *he'd been talking*

6. Hypercorrections (the use of *two* grammatical markers of the same type):
   likeded for *liked, helpeded* for *helped, stoppeded* for *stopped*

Of course the omission of such inflectional endings may occasionally reflect a lack of understanding, but such omission usually indicates simply that the reader has processed the meaning of the sentence and has then re-encoded that meaning into the syntactic pattern that he or she finds most natural. Such re-encoding is directly analogous to what the child Echo did when asked to repeat sentences like *The man who I saw yesterday runs fast*: she reproduced the essence of the propositions in her own kind of surface structure.

At least some research indicates that it is the best readers who produce the most dialect-based miscues, lending further support to the idea that good readers extract underlying propositions and their relationships *before* producing a surface structure (B. Hunt 1974-75). And as indicated earlier, this sequence is to a large extent true even of *beginning* readers, as long as they are operating on the hypothesis that reading means getting meaning.

Before discussing the role of grammar in assessing and assisting the reader, it might be well to restate some points about the reading process:

1. Basically, reading means getting meaning from printed matter.

2. Reading involves an active search for meaning, for the underlying propositions and their relations.

3. In this active search, readers use grammar and meaning both to predict what will come next and to confirm or correct their predictions.

4. Readers make at least some use of syntactic strategies in reading. That is, they use such signals as word order, word endings, and function words to group words into syntactic constituents. To the extent that such syntactic grouping is possible, it aids in the identification of propositions.

5. Readers also make at least some use of semantic strategies. That is, they use content words to build propositions that make sense and then predict the function words accordingly.

6. In sum, proficient reading involves using surface structure as a means for determining deep structure, *and* using deep structure as a means for determining surface structure.

7. Miscues that alter surface structure but preserve deep structure both confirm this view of the reading process and reflect reading at its most proficient.

Assessing and Assisting the Reader

The discussion in the preceding sections raises the question of how important grammar really is in reading and in helping children read.

This question will be of continued concern as we explore readers' use of syntax in reading, some problematic kinds of syntactic constructions, some of the difficulties involved in dealing with the syntax of literature, and various ways of assessing and assisting students' use of syntactic and semantic context in reading. Those interested in exploring such topics further might consult Weaver's *Psycholinguistics and Reading: From Process to Practice* (tentative title), forthcoming in 1979 from Winthrop Publishers.

Using and Coping with Syntax

Obviously we *do* use word order and, to a lesser extent, function words and grammatical endings as we read, but it is by no means certain that we need to *teach* children to do this. Indeed, in Weber's study (1970), about 90% of the first graders' miscues were grammatically acceptable with what preceded them in the sentence, while over 60% of the miscues were also grammatically acceptable with what followed; furthermore, this study included both good and poor readers (Weber 1970, pp. 153 and 160). Such data certainly calls into question the need for teaching children to use grammatical context as they read.

On the other hand, Weber's study did produce some evidence that the poorer readers were not using context as well as the better readers. There was a considerable difference in the correction of miscues that were *not* acceptable with following context. The better group corrected 85% of these miscues, while the poorer group corrected only 42% (p. 162). This suggests, then, that the nonproficient reader may need guidance and practice in identifying and correcting those miscues that are not grammatically acceptable with the context that follows. Such miscues are of necessity not *semantically* acceptable with the following context either; that is, they usually reflect a loss of meaning.

It would seem most economical, then, for teachers to use a single procedure to assess readers' use of both syntactic and semantic context. Nevertheless, it may sometimes be desirable to assess only the readers' ability to make intuitive use of grammar as they read. Passages with nonsense words are often good for this purpose. Most of the published examples seem to be for upper elementary school students or older, as with this excerpt from the "Crashe Helmutt" exercise in a junior high text (Lester 1973, p. 31). Basically, the students are asked to choose the most appropriate nonsense word to complete each sentence:

1. I _____ a movie on television last night.
   (*frabs, zinged, flumping, vorpous*)
2. Crashe Helmutt was the _____ of the movie.
   (*turgoons, frib, mogged, flonkish*)

3. He played the role of a _____ chifforobe salesman.
   (*yaggiest, nunky, mimpier, burfles*)
4. His wife, played by Wednesday Rivet, nagged him _____.
   (*ferd, mongous, zizzed, gabbingly*)

If students have trouble with such an exercise, teachers might construct or select similar materials to use instructionally. A good choice might be Lewis Carroll's "Jabberwocky," a perennial favorite for its imaginative use of language.

With junior high and older students, teachers might use O'Donnell's test for determining whether students can recognize certain kinds of syntactic alternatives (O'Donnell 1973). In each group of three sentences, students are to indicate the one that is *least* like the other two in "meaning":

1. a. The bindle saw the duplon.
   b. The duplon was seen by the bindle.
   c. The duplon saw the bindle.
2. a. The boskin that was sitting by the portis concealed the canis.
   b. The boskin sitting by the portis concealed the canis.
   c. The boskin was sitting by the portis that concealed the canis.
3. a. It was obvious that the kendis liked the dokis.
   b. The kendis that liked the dokis was obvious.
   c. That the kendis liked the dokis was obvious.
4. a. For the masil to see the femil was easy.
   b. It was easy for the masil to see the femil.
   c. For the femil the masil was easy to see.

For older students, tests like the above are especially useful in assessing the ability to handle some of the more complicated kinds of syntactic constructions, such as the nominalizations in the third and fourth groups of sentences. Again, teachers could use such activities for either assessment or instruction or both. Other useful "tests" are described in *Measures for Research and Evaluation in the English Language Arts* (Fagan, Cooper, and Jensen 1975); see especially the measures used by Marcus, Simons, Robertson, Montague, and Cosens. Some of these materials use nonsense words while others use only real words and sentences.

Various kinds of research indicate that, given two sentences that express the same propositions, one may be more difficult to process than the other. The sentences in O'Donnell's third and fourth sets above illustrate this point: people find it more difficult to process *That the kendis liked the dokis was obvious* than to process its synonymous counterpart, *It was obvious that the kendis liked the dokis*; similarly,

For the masil to see the femil was easy is more difficult to process than *It was easy for the masil to see the femil.* The more difficult sentences have nominalizations in subject position, and the listener or reader must hold the underlying propositions in mind until reaching the predicate (*was obvious, was easy*). It is easier for people to determine the underlying propositions when this simple "predicate" part comes first, followed by the complex nominalizations.

For adult and/or proficient listeners and readers, the difference may lie simply in reaction time: that is, it may simply take slightly longer to interpret the sentences that are grammatically more complex. For younger and/or less proficient listeners and readers, the more complex structures may be impossible to interpret correctly. Then, too, it may be that children who can interpret syntactically difficult constructions aurally may not yet be able to interpret all of them in print, especially if they tend to process words one at a time and/or if they do not operate upon the hypothesis that reading means getting meaning. In any case, teachers may find it useful to construct their own test to determine students' abilities to interpret some of the more difficult variants listed below. The "problem" construction is first explained and then illustrated along with a simpler, less difficult variant.

1. One difficulty is with constructions that require readers to hold all or part of one constituent in mind while processing another.
    a. Sentences with a relative clause embedded within a main clause are usually more difficult to process than sentences with the same ideas expressed in two main clauses. Thus sentence (1) below is more difficult than sentence (2):
        (1) The owl, who eats candy, runs fast.
        (2) The owl eats candy, and the owl runs fast.
    b. Sentences with an adverb clause before the main clause are usually more difficult to process than sentences with the main clause first. Thus sentence (1) below is more difficult than sentence (2) in each case:
        (1) Before you pick up the red marble, pick up the blue marble.
        (2) Pick up the blue marble before you pick up the red marble.

        Here, the first sentence is harder for another reason as well: the order of the clauses does *not* correspond with the temporal order of events.
        (1) Because he had lost the race, he stomped off the field.

(2) He stomped off the field because he had lost the race. Again, there is a second reason why the first sentence is harder: the cause is presented before the effect. (This effect-cause requirement seems to take precedence over the requirement that the order of the clauses should reflect the order of events.)

c. Sentences with a nominalization in subject position are usually more difficult to process than sentences with the nominalization in the predicate part of the sentence. Thus sentence (1) below is more difficult than sentence (2):

(1) To paint pictures is fun.

(2) It's fun to paint pictures.

d. Sentences with modifiers coming after the subject noun are usually more difficult to process than sentences in which the modified noun occurs in predicative nominative or direct object position. Thus sentence (1) below is more difficult than sentence (2) in each case:

(1) The man with the monkey is Mr. Harvey.

(2) Mr. Harvey is the man with the monkey.

(1) The house that overlooks the lake was just bought by Mr. Roberts.

(2) Mr. Roberts just bought the house that overlooks the lake. Here, the first sentence may be more difficult for another reason as well: it is passive rather than active (that is, it violates the "normal" agent-action-object order of words).

e. Sentences in which a verb-plus-particle construction is interrupted by a lengthy noun phrase are more difficult to interpret than sentences in which the particle immediately follows the verb. Thus sentence (1) below is more difficult to interpret than sentence (2):

(1) I hunted my old college roommate up.

(2) I hunted up my old college roommate.

f. Sentences with a long indirect object phrase and short direct object phrase are more difficult to interpret than sentences in which these elements are expressed as a short direct object phrase followed by a long prepositional phrase. Conversely, sentences with a long direct object phrase followed by a short prepositional phrase are more difficult to interpret than sentences in which these elements are expressed by a short indirect object phrase followed by a long direct object phrase. Thus sentence (1) below is more difficult than sentence (2) in each case:

(1) He gave the son who lives in California his stamps.

(2) He gave his stamps to the son who lives in California.

(1) He gave all the stamps he had ever collected to his son George.

(2) He gave his son George all the stamps he had ever collected.

2. Another difficulty is with constructions that are relatively inexplicit about specifying the underlying syntactic and/or semantic relationships.

   a. Sentences with nominal near-clauses are usually more difficult to interpret than sentences with full nominal clauses. Thus sentence (1) below is more difficult than sentence (2) in each case:

(1) He didn't remember having done it himself.

(2) He didn't remember that he had done it himself.

(1) He knew her to be angry.

(2) He knew that she was angry.

(1) Ask Mary what to feed the dog.

(2) Ask Mary what you should feed the dog.

   b. Sentences in which the performer of an action is not explicit are usually more difficult to interpret than sentences in which the performer is made explicit. Thus sentence (1) below is more difficult than sentence (2):

(1) It is easy to please Snoopy.

(2) It is easy for someone to please Snoopy.

   c. Sentences which do not include an optional syntactic marker may be more difficult to interpret than sentences which include the optional marker. Thus sentence (1) below may be more difficult than sentence (2) in each case:

(1) We took cookies to the little old lady down the street.

(2) We took cookies to the little old lady who lives down the street.

(1) They thought Sam should know the truth.

(2) They thought that Sam should know the truth.

Although it is uncertain to what extent the more difficult constructions above are likely to cause problems for readers, teachers may find it profitable to investigate at least some of these constructions with their own students. At the very least, teachers might keep alert for such constructions in the materials their students are reading, if only to determine whether the constructions are understood.

It is by no means clear how close the match needs to be between children's oral and/or written syntax and the syntax they are expected to process in reading. Nevertheless, the passages below may give teachers some idea of the kinds of syntactic constructions that are most appropriate for students at grades 4, 8, and 12. The passages are taken from Kellogg Hunt's research on sentence combining, and they indicate some of the syntactic constructions that are typical of children's writing at these three grade levels (Hunt 1970, pp. 64-67):

4th grade

Aluminum is a metal and is abundant. It has many uses and it comes from bauxite. Bauxite is an ore and bauxite looks like clay. Bauxite contains aluminum and it contains several other substances. Workmen extract these other substances from the bauxite. They grind the bauxite and put it in tanks. Pressure is in the tanks...

Children's free writing shows more syntactic variation than this sentence-combining exercise typically did, but here the children combined underlying propositions (basic "kernel" sentences) mainly by conjoining two clauses within one sentence (*it has many uses and it comes from bauxite*).

8th grade

Aluminum is an abundant metal, has many uses, and comes from bauxite which is an ore that looks like clay. Bauxite contains several other substances. Workmen extract these from bauxite by grinding it, then putting it in pressure tanks...

The noteworthy features here are the compound predicate (*is an abundant metal, has many uses, and comes from bauxite*); the full relative clauses (*which is an ore, that looks like clay*); and the gerundives (*by grinding it, then putting it*).

12th grade

Aluminum is an abundant metal with many uses. It comes from an ore called bauxite that looks like clay. It contains aluminum and several other substances which are extracted from the bauxite. They grind the bauxite and put it in pressure tanks.

The noteworthy features here are the reduced relative clauses (the adjectival phrases *with many uses* and *called bauxite*) and the full and reduced passives (*which are extracted from the bauxite* and *called bauxite*).

Superior adult writers (for comparison)

Aluminum, an abundant metal of many uses, is obtained from bauxite, a clay-like ore. To extract the other substances found in bauxite the ore is ground and put in pressure tanks.

Here, two more clauses have been reduced to adjectival phrases, specifically appositives (*an abundant metal of many uses* and *a clay-like ore*). Similarly, the number of full and reduced passives has been increased to four (*is obtained from bauxite, found in bauxite, the ore is ground and put in pressure tanks*). Also, there is an adverbial of purpose (*To extract the other substances found in bauxite*).

It would be dangerous to assume that there is a one-to-one correspondence between the kinds of constructions written in this experiment and the kinds of constructions best understood by children at these respective grade levels. On the other hand, one general principle should be clear from these examples: the younger the writer, the less able he or she is to combine underlying propositions into a tight, succinct surface structure. Therefore it seems reasonable to suppose that the younger the reader, the less able he or she will be to interpret sentences with a high degree of syntactic density, that is, with the underlying propositions reduced and condensed into a relatively succinct surface structure.

Much of this is obvious to the experienced teacher, of course, and if children are reading for meaning, then teachers may need to spend relatively little time helping them learn to determine underlying propositions from the syntax of ordinary prose. But what of literature? That may indeed be another matter.

Consider first the matter of poetry. One problem is that students typically have trouble determining the sentences of poetry and the underlying propositions that are expressed. Take, for example, the following poem from E. E. Cummings's *Collected Poems* (New York: Harcourt Brace Jovanovich 1963, Poem 13):

> the hours rise up putting off stars and it is
> dawn
> into the street of the sky light walks scattering poems
>
> on earth a candle is
> extinguished   the city
> wakes
> with a song upon her
> mouth having death in her eyes
>
> and it is dawn
> the world
> goes forth to murder dreams....
>
> i see in the street where strong
> men are digging bread
> and i see the brutal faces of
> people contented hideous hopeless cruel happy
>
> and it is day,
>
> in the mirror

i see a frail
man
dreaming
dreams
dreams in the mirror

and it
is dusk   on earth

a candle is lighted
and it is dark.
the people are in their houses
the frail man is in his bed
the city

sleeps with death upon her mouth having a song in her eyes
the hours descend,
putting on stars....

in the street of the sky night walks scattering poems

First of all, children may need help in determining the surface sentences of the poem (indeed, many students seem not to know that poems even contain sentences!). Second, children may need some help in determining the underlying propositions. Consider, for example, the italicized constructions below:

into the street of the sky light walks *scattering poems*
. . . .
. . . . the city
wakes
with a song upon her
mouth *having death in her eyes*

Will students automatically realize that it is the light which is scattering poems, or that it is the city which has death in her eyes? Possibly not: students may need help in determining these underlying propositions. However, this does *not* necessarily mean that students need to know participial phrases. In fact, the most helpful way to prepare students to understand such constructions may be through sentence-combining exercises, in which grammatical terminology does not necessarily have to be used. Suppose, for example, that students had been given practice in combining sentences to form full relative clauses and then to reduce these to participial phrases:

Matrix: the city wakes.

Insert: The city has death in her eyes.

Results: The city, *who has death in her eyes*, wakes.
The city, *having death in her eyes*, wakes.
The city wakes, *having death in her eyes*.
Having death in her eyes, the city wakes.

Students who have had practice in creating such sentences should find them easier to understand in their reading, and indeed there is some evidence suggesting that a substantial amount of sentence-combining practice aids reading comprehension (see Hughes 1975). But in any case when students *do* have trouble understanding the sentences of literature, the teacher does not necessarily have to use grammatical terminology in giving them assistance. The best procedure may simply be to show how the sentence could have been created from the underlying sentences.

In fact, this kind of teaching strategy needs to be employed far more often than we may realize. Minkoff and Katz, for example, note that students often have difficulty with certain kinds of syntactic constructions, particularly in older literature like *Tom Sawyer*. Following are some of the examples cited throughout Minkoff and Katz's article (1973):

> He felt much as an astronomer feels who has discovered a new planet.
>
> The truth was that a superstition of his had failed here which he and all his comrades had always looked upon as infallible.
>
> ...where the western boys ever got the idea that such a weapon could possibly be counterfeited to its injury is an imposing mystery...
>
> The Red-Handed made no response, being better employed.
>
> These two commanders did not condescend to fight in person—that being better suited to the smaller fry...

In these cases as well as in many others, the surface structure tends to obscure the deep structure, at least for students unfamiliar with these kinds of syntactic constructions. Teachers may need to give students direct help in determining the underlying propositions as well as indirect help via sentence-combining exercises, which will be discussed in the chapter on writing.

The other major problem with the syntax of literature is that it is often difficult to determine the basic elements of the underlying propositions. That is, it may be difficult to determine who or what is the agent or experiencer, who or what is the goal or object of the action, what is the instrument of the action, and so forth. This difficulty is particularly common with older literature, as in these examples from an article by Chatman, "Linguistics and Teaching Introductory Literature" (1956-57):

> The God who darts around the world his rays
> Swift on his sooty pinions flits the gnome
> What moved my mind with youthful lords to roam

Once again, teachers do not really need grammatical terminology to help students understand such constructions. Indeed, the easiest method is probably to ask a series of questions such as these:

1. In *The God who darts around the world his rays,* who or what is doing something? (God, the God.) What is this God doing? (Darting his rays.) Well, where is he darting them? (Around the world.)

2. In *Swift on his sooty pinions flits the gnome,* who or what is doing something? (The gnome.) What is he doing? (Flitting.) How is he flitting? (Swift on his sooty pinions.)

3. In *What moved my mind with youthful lords to roam,* who or what did something? (My mind.) What did it do? (It roamed.) With whom did it roam? (With youthful lords.)

Obviously, there will still be problems with unfamiliar words, but in getting at the underlying elements of propositions, teachers may well find *whodunit*-type questions more useful than grammatical terminology. Teachers need to draw out students' intuitive understanding of grammar more than to teach grammar as a system.

Using Syntactic and Semantic Context

But what of the less proficient reader who couldn't begin to read most of the literature that we have just discussed? Before examining how teachers can assess such students' needs and assist them, let us consider the characteristics typical of a good reader, compared with some of the characteristics typical of a poor reader (Weaver 1977, pp. 883-884).

In general, the good reader tends to predict what's coming next, to make miscues that preserve grammar and meaning and leave these uncorrected, and to correct those few miscues that don't fit in context. The following excerpt from a reading miscue analysis illustrates these strategies typically employed by the good reader, in this case a sixth-grader (the passage is from an O. Henry story, "Jimmy Hayes and Muriel," Porter 1936, p. 670). Underlining indicates the extent of a repetition, while ☺ indicates that the miscue was corrected. The other markings have the same meaning as before: a carat points to an insertion, a circle indicates an omission, ∩∪ indicates a reversal, and one or more words simply written above the text indicate a substitution. Each miscue or set of related miscues is numbered for later analysis (see p. 46):

After a hearty supper Hayes joined the smokers *around* ① about the fire.

His appearance did not *at all* ② ∧ settle all the questions in the minds of his brother rangers. They saw ~~simply~~ a loose, lank youth *young* ④ with tow-

colored sunburned hair and a berry-brown, *ingenious* ⑤ ingenuous face that

wore a quizzical, good-natured smile.

"Fellows," said the new ranger, "I'm goin' to interduce you to a

lady friend of mine. Ain't ⑥ever heard ⑦anybody call her ⓐ beauty, *much about*

but you'll all admit she's got *a* ⑧ some fine points about her. Come

along, Muriel!"

He held open the front of his blue flannel shirt. ⓒ Out ⑨of it

crawled a horned frog. A bright red ribbon was tied jauntily around *toad* ⑩

its spiky neck. It crawled to its owner's knee and ⑫ *it* sat there *the* ⑪

motionless.

"This here *'s* ⑬ Muriel," said Hayes, with an oratorical wave of his

hand, "has got *she's* ⑬ qualities. She never talks back, she always stays ⑭at

home, and she's satisfied with one red dress for everyday and

Sunday, too."

"Look at that blame *d* ⑮ insect!" said one of the rangers with a grin.

"I've seen plenty of them horny *toads* ⑯ frogs, but I never knew anybody to

have one ⓒ for a ⑰side partner. Does the blame thing know you from

anybody else?"

"Take it *her* ⑱ over there and see," said Hayes.

Despite the numerous miscues, this child is obviously using good
reading strategies.

Unlike the good reader, the poor reader tends to:

1. read one word at a time, treating each word as if it existed in
   isolation;

2. try unsuccessfully to sound words out, or make guesses, rever-

sals, and habitual associations, all with little regard to context (*souts* for *shouts*, *expert* for *except*; *with* for *rides*; *was* for *saw*; *can* for *and*);

3. ignore miscues that fail to preserve grammar and/or meaning.

These observations suggest, then, that what poor readers usually need is help in attending not just to grammatical context, but to semantic context as well. Indeed, readers' miscues are grammatically acceptable in context far more often than they are semantically acceptable (Goodman and Burke 1973).

How, then, to assess a reader's needs? The best way is surely to examine his or her miscues in context. (For a more thorough discussion, see Burke 1973, Y. Goodman and C. Burke 1972, and Weaver, forthcoming.) Basically, teachers need to find out three things:

1. Does the reader use preceding syntactic and semantic context to predict what is coming next?

2. Does the reader use following syntactic and semantic context to confirm or reject these predictions?

3. Does the reader correct (or attempt to correct) those miscues that don't fit in context?

Figure 2 presents a miscue analysis form that can be used for examining the reader's miscues; for illustration, I have analyzed the miscues on the passage about Muriel the frog (p. 46). Each time the reader departs from the text, the teacher should record what the text said and what the reader said. For each miscue, look first at how it fit with the preceding context. If it fit both syntactically and semantically with what came before, put a check in the "yes" column; if it fit syntactically but not semantically with what came before, put a check in the next column; if it fit semantically but not syntactically with what came before, put a check in the third column; and if it fit neither syntactically nor semantically with the preceding context, put a check in the "no" column. The other three questions can be handled similarly. If fewer than two-thirds of the miscues are in the "yes" column for any one of the questions, then examine the data further to see what kind of help the reader needs.

An illustration may help. In analyzing Jay's miscues on the passage about Muriel, we find that 100% of the miscues fit with the preceding context and 88% fit with the following context (though the miscues "ingenious" for *ingenuous* and "toad(s)" for "frog(s)" do change the meaning). Furthermore, although only 17% of the miscues were corrected, this low percentage of correction certainly does not indicate a

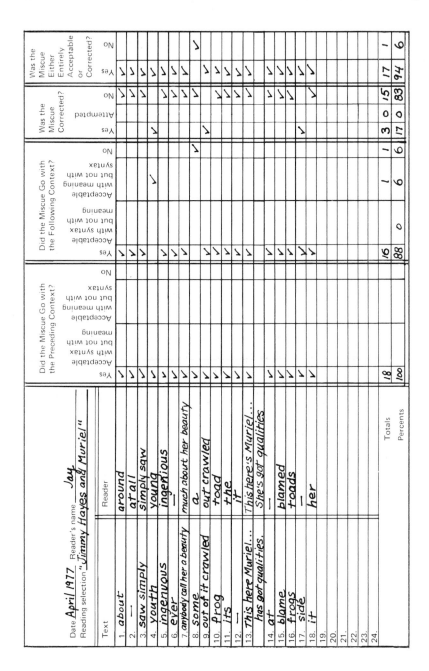

Figure 2.   Reading Miscue Analysis.

problem, because a total of 94% of his miscues were either entirely acceptable or corrected. Clearly, Jay does not need instruction in how to use context as he reads.

On the other hand, suppose that only 40% of a reader's miscues fit with the preceding context, and only 20% fit with the following context. Clearly, this reader would need help in using preceding context to predict what is coming next and help in using following context to confirm or correct such predictions. But does the reader need help in using syntactic context, semantic context, or both? A look at the other columns under "preceding context" and "following context" should provide the answers.

After teachers have done even a few thorough analyses of a reader's miscues, they often find it possible to make a quick but fairly sound analysis of a reader's miscues during an ordinary read-aloud session. For the teacher's records, it may be helpful to use a checklist something like the following:

1. Does the reader use preceding context to predict what is coming next?

   _____ yes _____ sometimes _____ no
2. Does the reader use following context to confirm or reject predictions?

   _____ yes _____ sometimes _____ no
3. Does the reader correct those miscues that don't make sense?

   _____ yes _____ sometimes _____ no

Such a checklist should be useful in determining a reader's strategies and needs.

In addition to analyzing reading miscues, the teacher might employ an individual or group "test" to gain insight into how well the students use preceding context to predict, and following context to confirm or reject, these predictions. The best kind of test for this purpose is the *cloze* test, developed by Wilson Taylor in 1953. The cloze procedure is based upon the assumption that language is redundant, that about one out of every five words in a stretch of text can be predicted from context. Hence the basic cloze procedure involves filling in every fifth word that has been omitted from a text. To see how the procedure works, try filling in the following blanks yourself (from Bormuth 1975, p. 70):

The Beaver

Indians call beavers the "little men of the woods." But they ____ really so very little. ____ beavers grow to be ____ or four feet long ____ weigh from 30 to ____ pounds. These "little men ____ the woods" are busy ____ of the time. That ____ why we sometimes say, "____ busy as a beaver."

___ know how to build ___ that can hold water. ___ use their two front ___ to do some of ___ work. Cutting down a ___ with their four sharp-___ teeth is easy. A ___ can cut down a ___ four inches thick in ___ 15 minutes.[11]

Doubtless you quickly learned to use not only preceding context but *following* context, and students being asked to do a cloze exercise should be advised to do the same. Doubtless you also realized that the ability to put a reasonable answer in some of the blanks depends in part upon your knowledge of beavers; hence if a cloze exercise is to test students' basic reading ability, the material must be on a topic familiar to them.

The answers to a cloze exercise can be evaluated in various ways, depending on the teacher's purpose. To get only a rough idea of the reader's ability to use context in reading, it would be sufficient to simply score the answers as to "right" or "wrong," accepting only those answers which exactly match the deleted word (but ignoring minor misspellings). If such a scoring procedure is used, the percent right will be relatively low: 44% on a cloze test is roughly equivalent to 75% on a standardized reading test, and 57% on a cloze test is roughly equivalent to 90% on a standardized test (Bormuth 1968, p. 433). But of course for diagnostic purposes it would be better to accept reasonable synonyms as well as an answer that exactly matches the deleted word. And ideally, teachers should examine each answer to see whether it fits with the preceding syntactic and semantic context and whether it fits with the following syntactic and semantic context. Such an analysis should enable the teacher to determine precisely what kinds of problems the student has in using context.

If indeed the teacher finds that a student or group of students needs help in learning to use context, one excellent instructional activity is the cloze procedure itself. In fact, one of the virtues of the cloze procedure is its versatility: it can be used to diagnose reading difficulties; to assist readers in learning to formulate, test, and confirm or correct hypotheses as they read; to test readers' comprehension; and to determine the suitability of reading materials for a given group of students (see Bormuth 1975, especially concerning readability). Instructionally, one advantage of the cloze procedure is that it forces readers to deal with both grammar and meaning. Another advantage is that it can be done orally as well as in writing, and hence the procedure (or some variant of it) can be used even with prereaders, beginning readers, and extremely poor readers. Still another advantage is that it can be varied to suit the particular needs of students (see Culhane 1970) and can be used in a variety of instructional settings, from large group to individual. The most important steps are these (see Bormuth 1975 for more detail):

1. Choose the passage to be used. If your aim is to create the "standard" kind of cloze test, choose a passage somewhat longer than 250 words. The topic should ordinarily be familiar to the student(s).

2. Type the passage, leaving the first and last sentences intact. Choose one of the first five words in the second sentence, and replace it with a blank fifteen spaces in length; thereafter, replace every fifth word with a fifteen-space blank, until you have typed fifty blanks. (One variation of this would be to provide the initial letter of the missing word.)

3. Have students discuss the reasons for their answers. This is vital, whether the exercise is done orally or in writing. Formal scoring is not necessary, unless the exercise is to be used as a test. Even then, it would be wise to accept synonyms for the missing word.

Perhaps the easiest way to prepare a useful set of cloze exercises would be to work from one or more published sets of "graded" materials.

The following kinds of activities might also be useful for classes and groups of students who need help in becoming more aware of their own intuitive knowledge of grammar and more conscious of how this knowledge can help them in reading (Weaver 1976; see Martin and Brogan 1975 for most of the underlying ideas).

1. *Substituting* one word or construction for another
    Put a sentence on the board and have children suggest substitutes for one of the words, or perhaps for more than one. Example of the kind of results you might get:

There was an old woman

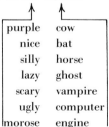

2. *Expanding* sentences
    Put a sentence on the board and have children suggest modifiers to put in one or more locations. Examples:

There was a(n) ___ old woman ___.

crotchety	who lived in a shoe
ugly	who lost her left shoe
funny	who baked cookies for Santa
sweet	who swallowed a flea

3. *Reducing* sentences to their basic subject and verb plus obligatory complement or modifier

   Put a sentence on the board and have children decide what parts can be crossed out without destroying the basic message of the sentence. Examples:

   We played ball yesterday.
   The man who had been hit in the head had to lie down.
   Tired and hungry, the old man crawled into bed, pulling the covers up to his chin.

4. *Rearranging* sentences

   Put a sentence on the board and have children suggest ways of rearranging the parts without changing the meaning. (Slight internal changes may be necessary, as illustrated here.) Then have the children discuss which version(s) they prefer and why. Examples:

   Tired and hungry, the old man crawled into bed, pulling the covers up to his chin.
   The old man was tired and hungry. He crawled into bed and pulled the covers up to his chin.
   Pulling the covers up to his chin, the old man crawled into bed. He was tired and hungry.
   The tired, hungry old man crawled into bed, pulling the covers up to his chin.

5. *Chunking* sentences

   Type up or put on the board a passage of prose having the same line divisions as the original. Then have students "chunk" the passage into units. These units will probably be grammatical constituents of one sort or another and will reflect what the students view as chunks of meaning. Naturally there is likely to be healthy disagreement as to how the passage should be chunked. Following is an example from Martin and Brogan (1975, p. TE 59):

CHICAGO, Jan. 20—One of the worst storms in memory hit Montana, eastern Washington, Utah, Nevada, Wyoming, Colorado and the Dakotas today in the form of blizzards, floods and bitter Arctic cold.

Some areas were buried under as much as 80 inches of snow, which forced the closing of schools and blocked highways. Freezing winds blew roofs off buildings, smashed windows and ripped down power and telephone lines. Brief gusts of the blizzard winds reached speeds as high as 95 miles an hour in parts of Montana and the Dakotas.

CHICAGO, Jan. 20—
One of the worst storms in memory
hit Montana,
eastern Washington,
Utah,
Nevada,
Wyoming,
Colorado
and the Dakotas today
in the form of blizzards,
floods
and bitter Arctic cold.
Some areas were buried
under as much as
80 inches of snow,
which forced
the closing of schools
and blocked highways.
Freezing winds
blew roofs off buildings,
smashed windows
and ripped down
power and telephone lines.
Brief gusts of the blizzard
winds
reached speeds
as high as
95 miles an hour
in parts of Montana
and the Dakotas.

6. *Avoiding habitual associations*

For common "habitual associations" and/or for readers who habitually confuse two words, write a passage in which both grammar and meaning strongly signal the word intended (Y. Goodman and C. Burke 1972). If a reader commonly reads *can* for *and* and vice versa, for example, one might construct a passage beginning as follows:

Jim called and asked his friend Bob, "Can you come to the fort today?" Bob answered, "Yes, I can. But let's go get some pop and cookies to take with us."

Obviously, most of these activities involve meaning as much as grammar, and this is doubtless as it should be.

In the Teacher's Edition section of each of their *Sounds of Language* readers, Martin and Brogan discuss the value of using literary materials with patterns that encourage semantic predicting and, inevitably, syntactic predicting as well. The following patterns of sequencing are discussed:

1. repetitive sequence,
2. cumulative sequence,
3. interlocking sequence,
4. familiar cultural sequence (cardinal and ordinal numbers, days of the week, months of the year, etc.),
5. chronological sequence,
6. problem-centered sequence,
7. rhyme-rhythm sequence.

The books in the *Sounds of Language* series (grades K-8) are replete with literary selections illustrating these predictable patterns. One example is "Over in the Meadow," which begins as follows:

> Over in the meadow
> in the sand
> in the sun
> Lived an old mother turtle and her little turtle one.

The selection illustrates several kinds of sequences: repetitive, cultural, and rhythm and rhyme. After the first three verses of the rhyme, Martin and Brogan give children clues to help them figure out how the rest of the rhyme goes (see Martin and Brogan's *Sounds of a Powwow* 1974, pp. 62-73):

1. The first four words of each verse are exactly the same.
2. The next few words tell where the creatures live.
3. The next few words tell who the mother is and how many babies she has.
4. The mother tells the babies to do something and they obey.
5. The verse ends by repeating what the babies did and where they were.

Each successive stanza is written with fewer and fewer words included, until finally with verse 10 there is just a picture of a mother beaver saying "Beave," accompanied by this stanza frame:

> ____ ____ ____ ____
> ____ ____ cozy wee den
> ____ ____ ____ ____ ____
> ____ ____ ____ ____ ____.
> "____," ____ ____ ____.

"____ ____," ____ ____ ____.
____ ____ ____ ____ ____
____ ____ ____ ____ ____.

Of course this one delightful example illustrates only a few kinds of predictability. Work with poetry (traditional and otherwise) needs to be balanced by work with prose, where students can gain practice in predicting from character, setting, plot, and so forth (for some specific ideas, see Stauffer and Cramer 1968). The mystery story is particularly useful for this purpose, as is the traditional folktale.

Folktales are especially valuable because they often contain so many predictable patterns and because they can be used with all ages. Take, for example, the tale of "The Fisherman and His Wife." One might begin by using a modified cloze procedure on the first paragraph, with blanks replacing just certain key words (Grimm Brothers 1945):

> There once was a fisherman who lived with his _____ in a miserable little _____ close to the sea. He went to fish every day, and he fished and fished, and at last one day as he was sitting looking deep down into the shining _____, he felt something on his line. When he hauled it up, there was a big _____ on the end of the line.

One variation would be to supply the initial letter and/or sound of each missing word. After students explain the reasons for their answers, the teacher could help them compare their choices with the words of the original: *wife, hovel, water,* and *flounder.*

From the very first paragraph we can begin to speculate about the role that the flounder will play in the story (Weaver 1977, pp. 884-886). When we learn that the flounder is an enchanted prince, we naturally expect something mystical and magical to happen—and it does, after the wife sends her husband back to ask a favor of the fish. First he gives her a pretty little cottage, then a big stone castle, and then—we are prepared to predict an even bigger and better dwelling. This indeed is what the woman receives, when the flounder grants her wish to be king. What else could the woman want? Perhaps to be God?

We are prepared for the wife's eventual downfall by the progressively deteriorating condition of the natural elements. When the fisherman first asks the flounder to give them a pretty little cottage, the sea has already begun to deteriorate: it is no longer bright and shining, but dull and green. By the time he asks that his wife be made king, the sea is dark, gray, rough, and evil-smelling. And conditions keep getting worse, until finally the woman is sent back to her old hovel.

This brief discussion indicates, then, that the tale of the fisherman and his wife lends itself to predicting through sentence structure, plot, characterization, setting, sequence, archetypal pattern, and other aspects of meaning. The classroom techniques can be equally various. First, the story can be read *to* students, or *by* students. With either approach, the reading can be stopped at intervals for the students to predict what's coming next and to discuss and justify their predictions. What do they think the wife will ask for next? How do they think the sea will look the next time the fisherman asks a favor? What do they think will happen when the woman asks to be made Lord of the Universe? Students can be invited to respond to such questions through discussion and/or by drawing, dictating, writing, or dramatizing their predictions.

Students who have learned to *predict*, to use experience and context *first*, are well on their way to being proficient readers. As Constance McCullough noted in her 1975 presidential "State of the Art" letter to members of the International Reading Association:

> The reading process appears to include active consideration of the meaning of what has been read and concern for what will be encountered; raising one's own questions, forming expectations of ideas to come, correcting interpretations when the expected does not occur, proceeding to new expectations and new questions, seeing pattern in the author's design of thought and expression, and predicting how the pattern will be extended.

It is becoming increasingly clear that even the beginning reader must establish these habits if he or she is to become a good reader.

Summary

The previous section demonstrated, to a limited extent, the fact that proficient readers formulate hypotheses about what is to come, then test and confirm or correct these hypotheses as necessary. We have indicated that the poor reader is often one who does not predict, does not anticipate what is coming next, but instead treats each word as if it existed in isolation. Even more often, the poor reader fails to use following context to detect and correct his or her miscues. Thus poor readers may need help in using syntactic and/or semantic context to predict, and even more likely, they may need help in using syntactic and/or semantic context to confirm or correct their predictions. Many readers do not seem to operate on the basic hypothesis that reading means getting meaning; at any rate, their miscues are more likely to be grammatically acceptable in context than to be semantically acceptable.

There are various means of assessing students' ability to employ intuitive knowledge of grammar as they read. One activity might require students to select an appropriate nonsense word to fit in a particular blank, while another activity might require students to determine which sentences have different surface structures but the same deep structure (that is, the same meaning). Certain kinds of syntactic constructions are more difficult to interpret than their synonymous counterparts, and students may need help in determining the deep structure from some of the more difficult variants. In dealing with the syntax of literature, students are likely to need help in determining what the underlying propositions are and help in determining the relationships among the words in these propositions. But in neither case does the teacher necessarily need to use grammatical terminology: for the most part, teachers can help students with the syntax of literature through sentence-combining and by asking *whodunit*-type questions.

To determine how well students can use both grammar and meaning to predict and confirm or correct as they read, teachers can analyze the students' actual reading miscues and/or examine their responses on a cloze exercise. The cloze procedure is, in fact, one of the best ways of helping readers who need to make more use of grammar and meaning as they read. Teachers can design various exercises focusing on syntax and/or semantics, but in the long run the most helpful procedure may be to select literature with predictable syntactic/semantic patterns of various sorts and to give students explicit guidance in using such patterns as they read. Such assistance should help students become better able to use surface structure as a means of determining deep structure *and* better able to use deep structure as a means of determining surface structure. In short, it should help students become more proficient readers.

4 Grammar and Writing

In the past two decades, much has been learned about writing and how it can be stimulated. The purpose here, however, is not to survey the considerable body of literature about writing but to discuss the role grammar might play in the teaching of writing. The discussion will deal first with developmental aspects of the writing process itself, then with various means of assessing and assisting the writer.

The Writing Process

Writing is primarily a process and only secondarily a product. But what is the purpose of this process? And what is its nature? Both questions are important for teachers.

Why do we write? Broadly speaking, we write in order to represent, clarify, and express our ideas and feelings to ourselves and to others. Writing is a way of coming to know, an interaction with one's own thoughts and emotions; it is also a way of communicating, a way of sharing those thoughts and emotions with others; and, finally, it is a way of creating, a way of giving artistic shape to one's perceptions and understandings. In James Britton's terms, these functions of writing are the *expressive*, the *transactional*, and the *poetic*, respectively (Britton 1970; see also Applebee 1977). Obviously, these functions are closely connected with the intended audience for whom one writes. Expressive writing is directed mainly toward the self, though it may be shared with a trusted adult or peer. Transactional writing is directed mainly toward someone else, and the audience may vary from specific (such as the teacher, one's classmates, a member of Congress) to general (such as those who read the "Letters to the Editor" column in the local newspaper). Somewhat similarly, poetic writing is ordinarily directed not merely toward the self, but toward a broader known or even unknown audience.

Beginning writers seem to operate upon the assumption that writing is *expressive* in function, that the purpose of writing is to express ideas for the writer's own satisfaction and perhaps for the satisfaction of a trusted adult. The child Natasha, for example, was satisfied that she had been able to write her own name when her mother sounded out the first line in figure 3 as "Sahspno" (Clay 1975, p. 3).[12] Despite the fact that the mother's rendition of the first line didn't sound much like "Natasha," and despite the imperfect correspondence between the sequence of letters and the sequence of sounds, the child was satisfied that she had managed to represent her own name in writing.

This expressive function is a natural consequence of children's ego-centrism in the pre-operational stage of intellectual development (up to about age 8). The child is primarily concerned with expressing meaning, his or her own meaning, and automatically expects this meaning to be understood. Just as in speech, children this age will write "this," "those things," and "the boy" without having previously made the referent clear. As the child matures beyond the pre-operational stage, the expressive function of writing tends to be manifested in this and other,

Figure 3.   "Sahspno."

more subtle ways. Here, for example, is a report by a ten-year-old boy (Britton 1970, pp. 178-179 in the Penguin Press edition, p. 14 in Larson):

How I Filtered My Water Specimens

> When we were down at Mr. Haris's farm I brought some water from the brook back with me. I took some from a shallow place by the oak tree, and some from a deep place by the walnut tree. I got the specimens by placing a jar in the brook and let the water run into it. Then I brought them back to school to filter....

After describing exactly what he did, the boy concludes:

> The experiment that I did shows that where the water was deeper and was not running as fast there was a lot more silt suspended as little particles in the water. You could see this by looking at the filter paper, where the water was shallow and fast there was less dirt suspended in it.

This writing seems to have an overriding transactional purpose, that of conveying the scientific results of the boy's experiment to an audience. Nevertheless, the passage contains several features which reveal an expressive function as well. The writer has conveyed not only the details crucial to the experiment but those relevant to his personal involvement in the experiment: Mr. Haris's farm, the brook, the oak tree, the walnut tree. The writer's transactional intent is modified somewhat by his personal involvement, his expressive need.

The writing should not be criticized because it does not represent a "pure" piece of transactional writing. On the contrary, it illustrates that most of the writing children do in the elementary years is likely to be expressive in function, or transitional between the expressive and the transactional or poetic (Britton 1970). In the secondary years, too, expressive writing is still important: it is valuable not only as a prelude or bridge to transactional and poetic writing but as an end in itself, a vital means of expressing and understanding one's own thoughts and feelings (see Gere 1977).

If the natural function of writing is expressive for most children, then we need to re-examine the role that "correct" mechanics should play in children's early writing. Consider, for example, the minimal performance objectives from the "Writing Skills" section of the *Minimal Performance Objectives for Communication Skills Education in Michigan*, published by the Michigan Department of Education in 1971. By the end of the *third grade*, learners are expected to demonstrate facility in writing by doing the following (pp. 28-29):

1. Learners will apply appropriate use of capitalization in their own writing.

2. Learners will apply appropriate uses of capitalization [punctuation?] in their own meaning in their own writing.
3. Learners will write complete sentences.
4. Learners will apply appropriate language usage in their own writing.
5. Learners will demonstrate knowledge of regularities of spelling patterns of the words they utilize in their writing.
6. Learners will produce written communications unique to the learner (e.g. description of observations, ideas, experiences, etc.).[13]

Even though these abilities were supposed to be measured against minimum criteria on an objectives-referenced test, the objectives themselves are still dangerously vague. But a more serious problem is that such expectations are contrary to the natural development of writing in the child. The young writer is more concerned with expressing ideas than with conveying those ideas to others; furthermore, the young writer finds it difficult to understand and adapt to the needs of an audience. Martin and Mulford put it this way (1971, pp. 382-383 in Larson):

> A seven-year-old is not much concerned with his reader beyond the fact that the writing is often seen as an "offering" to someone who is assumed to understand it just because *he* has written it. The child will not usually make any modification in what he writes, as an adult would, in order to communicate what he is saying. In short, he is writing above all for himself.... For a young child to put on record what he *wants* to say, to write so that his language closely fits himself, his experience, to his own satisfaction, seems to us to be skilled writing at this stage of his development....

What is "basic" for the young writer, then, is simply the expression of ideas and feelings. Only later will the child acquire a natural concern for conveying ideas to others, for communicating ideas through the transactional mode or evoking response through the poetic mode.

This point relates to the earlier suggestion that children may go through a series of hypotheses about the purpose and nature of writing:

1. Writing means expressing meaning in written language (that is, writing means expressing deep structure).

2. Writing means producing sequences of words with correct usage, sentence structure, punctuation, capitalization, and spelling (that is, writing means producing a "correct" surface structure).

3. Writing means using as many conventions of sentence structure,

usage, punctuation, capitalization, and spelling as necessary to convey meaning (that is, writing means using surface structure to convey deep structure).

The first hypothesis is the one natural to the young child: that writing means expressing meaning, primarily for oneself. The second hypothesis results from a premature attempt to get children to write for an audience and to write not only in such a way that their meaning is generally clear but to meet certain standards of "correctness." As early as the first grade, many children are already convinced of this second hypothesis, convinced that they can't write because they can't do it "right" (see Graves 1976).

Unfortunately, many students become so convinced of the second hypothesis that they never get form and meaning back together, they never become convinced that writing has any purpose other than to display their ability (or inability) to command various conventions of usage, sentence structure, capitalization, spelling, and the like.[14] They seldom if ever know the satisfaction of written self-expression, the pleasure of conveying thoughts or evoking feelings through writing.

The following list summarizes, then, some of the developmental aspects of the writing process:

1. Initially, writing means expressing meaning in written language.

2. Young writers are more concerned with expressing meaning for their own satisfaction than in conveying meaning to others or evoking a response to their verbal art. That is, they tend to see writing as expressive in function rather than transactional or poetic.

3. Young writers must to some degree "relearn" certain kinds of syntactic constructions as they attempt to express their underlying propositions in written language.

4. Young writers often make errors that are a sign of progress rather than of regression.

5. As young writers experiment more and more with the transactional and poetic functions of language, they increasingly understand the desirability of adjusting surface form to meet the needs and demands of an audience.

6. Finally, writing means using as many conventions of usage, sentence structure, punctuation, capitalization, and spelling as necessary to convey meaning.

An understanding of such developmental aspects is important if teachers are to make responsible decisions about the role of grammar in the writing curriculum.

Assessing and Assisting the Writer

Evaluating Writing

Although teachers may not directly "teach to the test," most are certainly inclined to teach what they think is worth testing. Consequently, it is important to look at the evaluation of student writing before developing a perspective on the role of grammar in the writing program. All too often, students' writing has been tested indirectly by standardized tests of usage, sentence structure, punctuation, capitalization, and spelling. At least testmakers recently have largely abandoned the items dealing merely with identification of subjects, predicates, adjectives, adverbs, and the like (see, for example, Sutton 1976). And some standardized tests do a reasonably good job of measuring students' abilities to deal with other aspects of writing besides mechanics; the STEP tests of writing (*Cooperative Sequential Tests of Educational Progress*) are one example (see Grommon 1976). But most standardized "writing" tests deal mainly with mechanics, which is disturbing for several reasons: (1) the use of such tests perpetuates the hypothesis that writing means producing written language which is superficially "correct";[15] (2) such tests tend to discriminate against those who speak a nonstandard dialect; (3) such tests measure only one broad aspect of writing, what might generally be called "mechanics"; and (4) there may be little correlation between scores on such a test and the overall quality of a person's writing.

Before protesting the cultural and social discrimination inherent in such standardized tests as the newly added usage section of the Scholastic Aptitude Test, the Conference on College Composition and Communication began its resolution as follows:

> RESOLVED, first, that CCCC protest the inclusion of an objective usage test in SAT, on the grounds that such tests are a measure of copyreading skill rather than a measure of student ability to use language effectively in connected discourse of their own composing; such tests place emphasis on mechanical matters of spelling, punctuation, and conventions of usage, rather than on clarity, appropriateness, and coherence of thought.... [16]

At the 1974 annual convention of the National Council of Teachers of English, a similar resolution was passed condemning such tests not only because of their inherent cultural and social bias but also because they encourage lopsided attention to only one aspect of writing.

Scoring high on a test of writing mechanics is not the same as writing well in a global sense, nor even the same as using good mechanics in one's own writing. Nevertheless, proponents argue that such tests usually correlate with overall writing ability. The Educational Testing Service claims, in fact, that in a 1975-76 study, its Test of Standard Written English correlated more closely with later writing performance than did a pre-instruction essay test (1977, p. 3). Diederich generalizes as follows (1974, p. 80):

> ... scores on a good objective test of English usage often correlate about .70 with averages of the two essay grades [on the kind of examination Diederich recommends]. It does not matter that they do not "really" measure "the same thing." If students who are good at one also tend to be good at the other, and vice versa, then it is a good indicator of proficiency in written English. Call it an editing test if you like, but I can promise you that students who do well on it also *tend to be* good writers.

However, I would insist it *does* matter that tests of mechanics and ratings of actual writing do not measure the same things. It does matter because the mere existence and use of such tests implies that "correct" mechanics is important in and of itself, and this in turn encourages teachers to teach mechanics in isolation from real writing.

The next section will present reasons for not teaching mechanics in isolation. Here, however, I wish to challenge Diederich's major conclusion, that there is a close correlation between tests of usage and ratings of actual writing. In fact, the writing evaluation program at Grosse Pointe, Michigan, has produced convincing evidence to the contrary. McCaig compared students' scores on standardized tests with the quality of their actual writing, evaluated on the following factors: ideas, sentence sense, unity, organization, coherence, sentence structure and wording, punctuation and capitalization, word choice, emphasis, spelling, and use of language (McCaig 1977b, p. 493). *Even though various aspects of mechanics were included among the factors evaluated*, there was no significant correlation between the ratings of the actual writing samples and the tests of punctuation, capitalization, usage, and "mechanics of Written English."

The message seems clear: if we want to evaluate students' writing, we must evaluate their writing! But how? The foregoing discussion of mechanics and the earlier discussion of developmental aspects of the writing process suggest some of the principles which might underlie a sound program for evaluating student writing (adapted in part from McCaig 1977). Specifically:

1. Such a program should take into account the fact that young writers progress only gradually from expressive to transactional

and poetic writing. Therefore, children should be evaluated only on the modes of writing most appropriate to their developmental level. Furthermore, meaning should be given considerably more emphasis than form, especially in the elementary grades.

2. Such a program should take into account what children meant to say or tried to do, in addition to what they actually did. McCaig and his evaluators coined the term "meaning unit" or "M-unit" to describe a word or group of words that can be reconstructed into a sentence in accordance with a judgment about the child's intention. The following are examples of first-grade M-units, reconstructed into "correct" sentences (McCaig 1972, p. 7):

Actual writing	*Adult's reconstruction*
Im gnu bren sum rock home	I'm going to bring some rocks home.
Owe ther was a littly girl	Once there was a little girl.
There was a machine nevrv stoop evn they trid	There was a machine that never stopped even though they tried.

In effect, an M-unit is a construction from which a reader can determine the underlying proposition(s), despite an immature or "incorrect" surface structure.

3. Such a program should take into account the fact that errors can be a sign of progress rather than of regression. Consider the earlier example of the writer just beginning to use adverb or adjective clauses; initially, he or she is likely to punctuate these as sentence fragments. Students should be rewarded for trying more sophisticated syntactic constructions rather than penalized for making errors in the process; similarly, students should be rewarded for trying to use more sophisticated vocabulary rather than penalized for misspelling such words.

4. Such a program should be multi-dimensional, evaluating not just mechanics but various aspects of writing. In analyzing evaluators' responses to a large set of essays, Diederich (1974) found five important factors: *ideas*; *mechanics* (errors); *organization*; *wording* (phrasing, vocabulary); and *flavor* (personal qualities). A model based upon such factors would treat mechanics as only one of five important aspects of writing.

5. Such a program should evaluate the student's writing according to specified criteria and/or according to the student's progress rather than in comparison with some sort of average or "norm."

An example of such a model of writing evaluation is discussed in McCaig 1972.

Mechanics

Putting "mechanics" in proper perspective does not remove the problem of how to help students learn accepted conventions of spelling, capitalization, punctuation, sentence structure, and usage. Obviously, grammar is of little help in teaching spelling, and not much more help in teaching capitalization (except, perhaps, as capitalization is interrelated with the punctuation of sentences). Traditionally, however, grammar has been considered helpful in teaching punctuation, sentence structure, and usage. Typically, teachers have taught grammar and (perhaps) the related rules of mechanics, marked up students' papers for not conforming to the rules, and bemoaned the students' failure to learn. And indeed, empirical research supports the feeling that little is gained from direct instruction in grammar and/or mechanics. Generally, there is not much more gained from corrective marks on students' papers. Edmund Farrell (1971, p. 141) reports the following letter from an English teacher:

> My own research has convinced me that red-inking errors in students' papers does no good and causes a great many students to hate and fear writing more than anything else they do in school. I gave a long series of tests covering 580 of the most common and persistent errors in usage, diction, and punctuation and 1,000 spelling errors to students in grades 9-12 in many schools, and the average rate of improvement in ability to detect these errors turned out to be 2 percent per year. The dropout rate is more than enough to account for this much improvement if the teachers had not even been there. When I consider how many hours of my life I have wasted in trying to root out these errors by a method that clearly did not work, I want to kick myself. Any rat that persisted in pressing the wrong lever 10,000 times would be regarded as stupid. I must have gone on pressing it at least 20,000 times without visible effect.

Unfortunately, this teacher's experience is all too common. There seems to be little value in marking students' papers with "corrections," little value in teaching the conventions of mechanics apart from actual writing, and even less value in teaching grammar in order to instill these conventions. Furthermore, students who *know* the accepted conventions of punctuation, sentence structure, and usage do not necessarily *follow* these conventions in their own writing. But the problem may lie primarily in the way teachers structure the writing experience.

Writing is a much more complex process than is commonly acknowledged in the classroom. Here, for example, Cooper and Odell describe the writing or "composing" process (1977, p. xi):

> Composing involves exploring and mulling over a subject; planning the particular piece (with or without notes or outline); getting started; making discoveries about feelings, values, or ideas, even while in the process of writing a draft; making continuous decisions about diction, syntax, and rhetoric in relation to the intended meaning and to the meaning taking shape; reviewing what has accumulated, and anticipating and rehearsing what comes next; tinkering and reformulating; stopping; contemplating the finished piece and perhaps, finally, revising. This complex, unpredictable, demanding activity is what we call the *writing process*. Engaging in it, we learn and grow.

In short, we might say that the writing process consists of at least three major stages: *prewriting, writing,* and *rewriting.*

One of the reasons why students have not applied their knowledge of writing conventions is that this three-stage process of prewriting, writing, and rewriting has often been foreshortened to just the middle stage, that of writing (Emig 1971). And, when composing a first draft, most writers tend to be much more concerned with expressing meaning than with conforming to standards of correctness. If students are not encouraged to revise and edit what they have written, they will never get to the stage when attention to surface detail is most relevant: the rewriting stage. It is in helping students rewrite, then, that teachers can most profitably turn students' attention to various aspects of mechanics (see, for example, either of Gebhardt's 1977 articles). Furthermore, students will profit much more from direct feedback and assistance in this rewriting stage than from any prior instruction in mechanics or any suggestions for consulting a handbook. The interaction with a genuine audience is crucial.

Even at the rewriting stage, however, it is vital that teachers avoid trying to get students to "correct" all the mechanical faults of their writing at once. Martin and Mulford offer some sage advice, and though their recommendations are for teachers of young writers in particular, the advice is pertinent to teachers at every level (Martin and Mulford 1971, p. 390, p. 388 in Larson):

> The teacher should select carefully from among the child's errors when he has made more than one or two, and should then regard his selections as one, relatively unimportant element in the matter to be discussed. What is fundamental is involvement by the teacher in the *substance* of the child's writing. Such involvement guarantees to the child that corrections are worth taking seriously....
> ... a teacher simply has to learn to judge how much concern for the conventions he can evince without it beginning to get in the way,

without it inducing in a child a false sense of priorities, or
confusion. This will vary, perhaps considerably, from child to
child—according to his age, his ability, his interest, his flexibility,
his aspirations; the effects of his past experience, of his parents'
expectations, of his friends' attitudes; his attitudes to reading, to
writing, to learning generally, to the teacher, to the school. . . . The
list could be much extended.

All of this suggests that the various conventions of the written language
can best be learned in the crucible of experience, when the writer is
seeking to meet the needs and demands of a real audience. In such a
context, it is usually easier to explain these conventions by means of
examples than by citing grammatical rules, complete with their seem-
ingly abstruse terminology.

In short, direct teaching of mechanics has perhaps no positive effect
at all unless certain conditions are met. First and foremost, the
instruction must meet a felt need on the part of the *students*. A small
minority of students will always be convinced that they need almost
anything the teacher sees fit to teach them. In that category would
probably fall most teachers who feel that the study of grammar was
beneficial. Unfortunately, however, many students do not have such
ready motivation. For them, the need must be more immediate, perhaps
spurred by a recent conference with the teacher. A related point is that
students should not be given direct instruction in aspects of mechanics
that they have already mastered, a point that may seem self-evident but
is all too often ignored in practice. Finally, the instruction must cover
neither too much nor too little. Students could hardly be expected to
master all aspects of punctuation at once, but if instruction is always
confined to something as limited as using commas to separate items in a
series, students may be able to exhibit the desired behavior only in the
context of an exercise.

Large-group instruction is almost inevitably unproductive because it
is rare that the students in a large group (such as an entire class) will all
feel the need for a particular kind of assistance at a given time. At least
once, however, I have felt successful in the attempt. One of my better
writers had brought to conference a good pair of objective and
subjective descriptions, poorly punctuated. With his permission I
prepared the paper for class discussion, omitting all capitalization and
punctuation. The writer himself was motivated, partly because he could
profit from his classmates' assistance before revising the paper to put in
his writing portfolio (besides, he was one of those rare students who do
expect to benefit from most instruction). Most of the class felt a general
need to learn more about punctuation, and they too could use their
increased insights to modify their own descriptions. The time was

unusually ripe for our "lesson" on punctuation. Here is the paper we discussed; there are two versions, an "objective" description and a "subjective" description:

> northern red oak it is approximately 50 feet tall and 30 inches in diameter its bark is dark brown to gray in color and very rough the leaves are 6 to 11 inches long with pointed tips the branches spread out near the middle making it about 30 feet wide the tree bears acorns which vary in size they are brown and green in color and have two parts to them the crown which is rough and bowl shaped and the seed which is smooth shelled with yellowish white meat

> our oak tree towering tall above everything around it the old oak spreads its branches majestically outward from its entwined roots deep in the earth to its uppermost leaf the oak shows signs of strength and age the bark is dark and rough with ridges running up its trunk like deep gorges in which the ants scamper about its wrinkled skin shows well the trees age but despite the ancient look of the bark its bright green leaves rustle against each other in the wind giving this giant a youthful look in the glowing sunlight its delightful fruit the acorn hangs gently but secure to the flexible branches like little soldiers with helmets they fall or are dropped from the heights by the hungry squirrels to the ground where they sink into the earth

Doubtless it would have been helpful if students had had a ready understanding of such terms as *clause* (independent and dependent), *subject*, *predicate*, and perhaps a few others. Most students did not have such an understanding, however, so I defined by example those few grammatical terms I felt compelled to use. Generally, however, we talked about such things as where the writer might want the reader to pause, which units seem to constitute a "sentence" (they had a good intuitive sentence sense), and which details seemed to belong together. Take, for example, these three ways of punctuating the first lines of the second description.

> Our oak tree, towering tall above everything around it. The old oak spreads its branches majestically outward, from its entwined roots deep in the earth to its uppermost leaf. The oak shows signs of strength and age.

> Our oak tree, towering tall above everything around it. The old oak spreads its branches majestically outward. From its entwined roots deep in the earth to its uppermost leaf, the oak shows signs of strength and age.

> Our oak tree. Towering tall above everything around it, the old oak spreads its branches majestically outward. From its entwined roots deep in the earth to its uppermost leaf, the oak shows signs of strength and age.

These combinations clearly do not exhaust the possiblities, but they were the ones that most readily suggested themselves. Any version, we realized, was bound to start with a group of words that was not a normal sentence—but *which* group of words? After discussing some of the possible ways of punctuating these lines, we tried to decide which one or ones were most desirable. Most of the class favored the third alternative, which includes the ideas of towering and spreading in one sentence and which most clearly indicates that all parts of the tree show its strength and age. Thus we were concerned not merely with grammar (however implicitly), but with rhetoric. As Christensen has said, "Grammar maps out the possible; rhetoric narrows the possible down to the desirable or effective" (Christensen 1967, p. 39). This is precisely what we tried to do.

To summarize, instruction in mechanics is most effective in the rewriting stage; such instruction is most effective in response to a need that the individual student recognizes; and such instruction is most effective when the use of mechanics is demonstrably relevant to effective communication. Furthermore, prior teaching of grammatical terminology is not necessary. Indeed, even when students *have* studied grammar, most are not able to remember the terminology and/or "rules" well enough to apply this knowledge to their own writing. Instead of teaching grammar as a prelude to writing, teachers will usually find it much more effective to introduce the bare necessities of grammatical concepts and terminology while helping students discover how their writing can be made more effective.

Sentence Combining

Is there any other use for grammar in the writing curriculum? As with reading, the answer seems to be that the formal study of grammar is of relatively little help to students, but a knowledge of grammar can help *teachers* in their efforts to improve student writing.

The good writer tends, first of all, to be a fluent writer; the good writer writes *more* than the poor writer. Also, the good writer tends to write sentences which are syntactically more mature. The term "syntactic maturity" refers to a relationship between deep structure and surface structure: a "syntactically mature" sentence expresses a relatively high number of underlying propositions in relatively few words. Thus syntactic maturity might be expressed as a ratio between the number of underlying propositions reflected in a given language sample and the number of grammatical sentences (T-units) the sample contains (see Calvert 1971, described in Fagan, Cooper, and Jensen 1975). Loban provides a concise description of how such syntactic maturity develops (Loban 1970, p. 625):

> As they [schoolchildren] mature, the low group increases its ability
> to use dependent clauses whereas the high group shifts to that
> tighter coiling of thought accomplished by infinitive clauses, parti-
> cipial, prepositional, and gerund phrases, appositives, nominative
> absolutes, and clusters of words in cumulative sentences.

Much of this development occurs quite naturally in speech and equally
naturally in writing—provided students are given plenty of opportunity
to write, and especially to write in the expressive mode where they may
feel freer to experiment (consciously or unconsciously) with different
kinds of syntactic constructions.[17] Nevertheless, the teacher can play a
vital role in stimulating children's use of their syntactic resources.

Much of the pioneering research in the area of syntactic maturity was
done by Kellogg Hunt. Although the most reliable measures of syntactic
maturity must doubtless take the relationship between deep structure
and surface structure explicitly into account (see above), Hunt found
that the best *simple* measure of syntactic maturity in normal free
writing is simply the average length of the grammatical sentence, or
"minimum terminable unit." This T-unit, as Hunt called it, consists of
an independent clause plus any dependent clauses or elements that may
be attached to or embedded within it. Not surprisingly, Hunt found that
older students tended to write longer T-units than younger students.
Here are his statistics for fourth graders, eighth graders, twelfth graders,
and some skilled adult writers who were published in *Atlantic Monthly*
and/or *Harpers* (Hunt 1965, p. 56):

	4th	8th	12th	Skilled Adults
Average (mean) no. of words per T-unit	8.60	11.50	14.40	20.30

Obviously "average T-unit length" is only a measure of surface structure,
but it reflects, albeit indirectly and imperfectly, the fact that older
writers tend to express more deep structure in a given amount of surface
structure. More mature writers tend to reduce full clauses to phrases
and single words, to engage in that "tighter coiling of thought" of which
Loban spoke. A good example is the typical rewriting of Hunt's sentences about aluminum (see pp. 39-40).

A more thorough look at Hunt's data is instructive. The number of
adverbial embeddings changed little from one group to another, but
nominal and adjectival embeddings increased with the maturity of the
writer. From Hunt's data, Mellon computed statistics on nominal and
adjectival embeddings (adapted from Mellon 1969, p. 19; see Table 1). As
far as one can tell, the greatest difference in the use of nominals was
between the eighth graders and the twelfth graders. The greatest

Table 1

Frequencies of Constructions per 100 T-units

Construction type	4th	8th	12th	Skilled Adult
Factive and WH-word nominals (clauses)	9	12	27	21
Gerundive and infinitival nominals (near-clauses)	6	10	23	not available
		greatest increase		
Adjectival clauses	5	9	16	25
Adjectival phrases	13	28	46	92
Adjectival words	33	68	81	152
			greatest increase	

difference in the use of adjectivals was between the twelfth graders and the skilled adult writers.

One of the conclusions which might reasonably be drawn from such data is this: that while mature use of nominals *may* be accomplished more or less naturally in writing, *students probably need direct assistance in learning to make effective use of the various kinds of adjectival constructions.*

The use of sentence-combining exercises seems to be one of the best ways of accomplishing this goal (see O'Hare 1973). Such exercises can be either oral or written, and either unstructured or structured. In unstructured exercises, the student is simply provided with two or more sentences to combine, with no explicit instructions as to how they should be combined. In structured exercises, the student is given directions as to how the sentences are to be combined and/or what kind of embedded structure should result. Below are two examples of the unstructured kind of exercise, followed by four examples of the more structured kind. For the structured exercises, there will be little variation in the possible results. For the unstructured exercises, considerable variation is possible.

Unstructured exercises

1. Sentences to combine

   There sits the ceramic toad.
   Its mouth is open wide in a grin.
   The grin is friendly.
   Its single eye is pleading for more food.

It eats objects.
The objects are small.
The objects are round.
The objects are made of metal.
The objects are pennies.
The objects are nickels.
The objects are dimes.
The objects are quarters.

The toad is not particular.
It eats anything it is offered.

Possible result

There sits the ceramic toad, its mouth open wide in a friendly grin, its single eye pleading for more food. It eats small, round, metal objects: pennies, nickels, dimes, and quarters. The toad is not particular, eating anything it is offered.

2. Sentences to combine

The skater stands up tentatively.
The skater is young.
His arms are stretched out like those of a tightrope walker.
His legs are stiff with fear.

Hesitantly, he moves one skate forward.
His other foot betrays him.
It moves too far backward.
Then he waves his arms wildly.
He lurches forward.
He falls.

Possible result

The young skater stands up tentatively, his arms stretched out like those of a tightrope walker, his legs stiff with fear. Hesitantly, he moves one skate forward. His other foot betrays him, moving too far backward. Then, waving his arms wildly, he lurches forward and falls.

Structured exercises

1. Sentences to combine (indicated by S), followed by the result (R).

S: The princess was determined to slay the dragon. The princess was brave. (*adjective*)

R: The brave princess was determined to slay the dragon.

S: Suddenly she caught sight of the dragon.
The dragon was lumbering over the hills. (delete *subject + be*)

R: Suddenly she caught sight of the dragon lumbering over the hill.

S: Then the dragon stood up tall.
His neck was stretched out to its full length (delete *be*)

R: Then the dragon stood up tall, his neck stretched out to
    its full length.

S: The princess knew *something*.
    The dragon would attack her soon. (*that*)

R: The princess knew (that) the dragon would attack her
    soon.

S: The princess was frightened.
    She had only a bow and arrow. (*because*)

R: The princess was frightened, because she had only a bow
    and arrow.

S: *Something* would be difficult.
    She would slay the dragon (*it* + *for-to*)

R: It would be difficult (for her) to slay the dragon.

S: But she must succeed.
    She must save the prince. (*why: for-to*)

R: But she must succeed in order (for her) to save the
    prince.

2a. Compare the ways of adding sentences in columns A and B.[18]

A	B
(1) I just walked along kind of slow-like and kicked any stones that were in my way.	I just walked along kind of slow-like, kicking any stones that were in my way.
(2) I turned and ran downstairs and thought I'd tell Mrs. Ennis.	I turned and ran downstairs, thinking I'd tell Mrs. Ennis.
(3) He paused and looked at the smoke.	He paused, looking at the smoke.

2b. Change each sentence below so it is added in the same way
     as the sentences are in column B above:

(1) We stood outside and waited for the fire engines.

(2) She ran to school and laughed all the way.

(3) Ronnie went to school and hoped Frazer would be there.

2c. Here are some short sentences. Rewrite each pair so that they
     look like the sentences in column A and then like those in
     column B.

(1) He ran to school. He thought he'd tell the teacher.

(2) Jane took the candy. She hoped no one saw her.

(3) Mr. Stoll drove a car. He thought it was faster than a train.

(4) Rita smiled brightly. She heard the telephone ring.

3. Compare the following ways of adding sentences: Joy smiled
    sweetly. She turned to her friend.

A	B
Joy smiled sweetly, turning to her friend.	Smiling sweetly, Joy turned to to her friend.

How is A different from B? Do the sentences mean the same thing? These ways of adding sentences involve changing one of the verbs to the -*ing* form. Notice that you always need a comma when you change the verb in the first sentence, as in the example under B.

Use -*ing* to add the following pairs of sentences as in A; then try to add them as in B. Can you always add sentences by changing the verb in the first sentence?

(1) The boys walked along the river. They watched the boats.

(2) Jack dashed for the subway. He panted as he ran.

(3) Jane was late for the party. She thought it started at eight o'clock.

What punctuation mark must you always use when you add the sentences as in the example under B?

4a. What are the three sentences that have been added to make this single sentence?

(1) I was in a swamp, water up to my middle, the sun going down.

Using sentence (1) as a model, add each of the following sentences in the same way:

(2) I was desperate. The sun was down. Indians were all around.

(3) George picked an apple. Its skin was rosy. Its leaves were green.

(4) They were hard times for Jamestown. Sickness was everywhere. Food was scarce. The Indians were unfriendly.

4b. These new sentence parts that you formed are called *absolutes*. In the last example there are three absolutes:

They were hard times for Jamestown, *sickness everywhere, food scarce, the Indians unfriendly.*

How are these absolutes formed? What change do you make when you add them? What punctuation do you use when you add them?

As the above examples suggest, unstructured exercises actually have a hidden structure, a certain logic of organization. However, they do not require explicit knowledge of grammar or grammatical terms. Furthermore, there is seldom a single "right" answer, and thus such exercises lend themselves well to a discussion of rhetorical effectiveness. Students can discuss not only what combinations are possible, but which combinations are most effective and why.

Structured exercises can have many variations as well. They can include practice in a variety of syntactic constructions, as does the exercise concerning the princess; or they can provide practice with only one or two kinds of constructions, as do exercises 2-4. Second, they can involve a moderate amount of labeling and/or grammatical terminology, as does the princess exercise; they can involve very little terminology and/or explanation, as do examples 3 and 4; or they can teach sentence combining entirely by example, as does exercise 2.

Both kinds of exercises lend themselves to a discussion of appropriate and effective punctuation.

Teachers who want to incorporate sentence combining into the curriculum might begin by assessing their students' present sentence-combining abilities and needs. One way to do this might be to use Hunt's "Aluminum" exercise, then compare the results with Hunt's original data. Here, for convenience, is Hunt's exercise (see Fagan, Cooper, and Jensen 1975, p. 201; see also Hunt 1970, pp. 64-65):

Aluminum

Directions: Read the passage all the way through. You will notice that the sentences are short and choppy. Study the passage, and then rewrite it in a better way. You may combine sentences, change the order of words, and omit words that are repeated too many times. But try not to leave out any of the information.

Aluminum is a metal. It is abundant. It has many uses. It comes from bauxite. Bauxite is an ore. Bauxite looks like clay. Bauxite contains aluminum. It contains several other substances. Workmen extract these other substances from the bauxite. They grind the bauxite. They put it in tanks. Pressure is in the tanks. The other substances form a mass. They remove the mass. They use filters. A liquid remains. They put it through several other processes. It finally yields a chemical. The chemical is powdery. It is white. The chemical is alumina. It is a mixture. It contains aluminum. It contains oxygen. Workmen separate the aluminum from the oxygen. They use electricity. They finally produce a metal. The metal is light. It has a luster. The luster is bright. The luster is silvery. This metal comes in many forms.

In this controlled writing experiment, Hunt found that the best measure of writing growth was the average clause length. Tables 2 and 3 show not only the average number of words per T-unit but also the average number of words per clause for the low, middle, and high groups in each grade studied, plus the available information for average and skilled adult writers (Hunt 1970, pp. 17-20). For convenience, the tables also present the comparable data from Hunt's earlier analysis of free writing (Hunt 1965, p. 56).

As is evident, the average number of words per T-unit was considerably less in the controlled sentence-combining experiment than in the free writing, which represented what writers normally do at their respective levels. The number of words per clause was also less in the controlled writing experiment. Consequently, teachers cannot expect a precise correlation between statistics derived from free writing and statistics derived from a controlled exercise, though clearly both kinds of data show the same developmental trends. More mature writers and more skilled writers at each grade level typically write longer T-units and longer clauses.

Many teachers will have neither the time nor the inclination to compile such data on their own students' writing, either their free writing or their response to a sentence-combining exercise. Still, teachers can get a general idea of students' sentence-combining abilities and needs simply by becoming aware of the syntactic structures in the

Table 2

Average Number of Words per T-unit

	Grade 4	Grade 6	Grade 8	Grade 10	Grade 12	Average Adults	Skilled Adults
			Free Writing				
	8.60	——	11.50	——	14.40	——	20.30
			Sentence Combining				
All groups together	5.42	6.84	9.84	10.44	11.30	11.85	14.78
Low group	5.23	5.73	7.55	9.61	10.17	——	——
Middle group	5.21	7.34	10.34	10.46	11.45	——	——
High group	5.81	7.47	11.66	11.66	12.30	——	——

Table 3

Average Number of Words per Clause

	Grade 4	Grade 6	Grade 8	Grade 10	Grade 12	Average Adults	Skilled Adults
			Free Writing				
	6.60	——	8.10	——	8.60	——	11.50
			Sentence Combining				
All groups together	5.19	5.76	6.79	7.35	7.85	8.40	9.95
Low group	5.04	5.31	6.09	6.87	7.42	——	——
Middle group	5.19	5.92	6.98	7.39	7.72	——	——
High group	5.33	6.05	7.30	7.81	8.39	——	——

students' usual writing, or by briefly looking over their responses to a sentence-combining instrument like that used by Hunt. Here, for example, are the partial responses of three different seventh-graders (Hughes 1975, pp. 29-30):

Student 1

Aluminum is an abundant metal. It has many uses. It comes from bauxite. Bauxite is an ore. Bauxite looks like clay. Bauxite contains aluminum. It contains several other substances. Workmen extract these other substances. They grind the bauxite. They put it in tanks. Pressure is in the tanks.

This writer combined only 12 of the underlying propositions (the original sentences) into his 11 T-units, a ratio of about 1 to 1, or 1.09 propositions per T-unit. The average number of words per clause is 4.64. The average number of words per T-unit is the same.

Student 2

Aluminum is abundant metal. It has many uses. It comes from an ore. The ore is called bauxite. It looks like clay. It contains aluminum. There are seven other substances that workmen extract from the bauxite. They grind the bauxite and put into pressured tanks. The other substances in the mass are removed by filters. A liquid remains and then they put it through seven other processes.

This writer's first 11 T-units contain the essence of 17 of the original sentences, a ratio of about 1½ to 1, or 1.55 propositions per T-unit. The average number of words per clause is 5.58. The average number of words per T-unit is 6.09.

Student 3

Aluminum is an abundant metal that comes from bauxite. Bauxite is an ore that looks like clay. Bauxite contains aluminum and several other substances. Workmen extract these other substances from the bauxite. Then the bauxite is ground and put in tanks that have pressure in them. They remove the mass other substances have formed with filters. The liquid that remains is put through several other processes. It finally yields a white powdery chemical that is alumina. It is a mixture that contains aluminum and oxygen. Workmen use electricity to separate the aluminum from the oxygen. They finally produce a light metal that has bright silvery luster.

This writer has combined 31 of the original 32 sentences into 11 T-units. (The original sentence "It has many uses" was omitted by the student.) Thus the student has condensed nearly three underlying propositions into each grammatical sentence, a ratio of nearly 3 to 1, or 2.82 propositions per T-unit. The average number of words per clause is 5.89. The average number of words per T-unit is 9.64.

Statistics concerning the average number of words per clause and per T-unit have been provided for comparison with Hunt's data. It is also interesting to compare these seventh graders' average number of propositions per T-unit with Hunt's data for various ages (1977):

Average Number of Propositions per T-unit

Grade 4	Grade 6	Grade 8	Grade 10	Grade 12	Skilled adults
1.1	1.6	2.4	2.8	3.2	5.1

With 1.09 propositions per T-unit, Student 1 resembles an average 4th grader; with 1.55 propositions per T-unit, Student 2 resembles an average 6th grader; and with 2.82 propositions per T-unit, Student 3 resembles an average 10th grader in sentence-combining ability.

Such a thorough analysis is seldom necessary for the classroom teacher, however. Even a cursory glance at these sentence-combining results would reveal that the first student has done almost no combining of sentences, the second student has been moderately successful in combining sentences, and the third student has been highly successful, at least for a 7th grader. Teachers should find it relatively easy to make such judgments about their own students' response to a sentence-combining exercise.

Interestingly, sentence-combining ability correlates with reading ability. In Hughes's study (1975), for example, students who initially showed low, middle, and high sentence-combining ability tended to be in the low, middle, and high reading groups respectively, according to various measures of reading comprehension. Furthermore, Hughes found that although the low sentence-combiners required prolonged and detailed help with sentence-combining exercises, in the long run their reading comprehension profited the most from such activity.

Once having made a general determination of students' sentence-combining abilities and needs, teachers still need to make several kinds of instructional decisions, such as:

1. What kinds of exercises are appropriate for the students' level of development?

2. Should such exercises cover a variety of syntactic constructions, emphasize only a few kinds of constructions, or both? In any case, how should they be sequenced?

3. Should sentence combining be done apart from normal writing, in conjunction with it, or both?

4. Should such exercises be written or oral or both?

5. Should such exercises be structured, unstructured, or both? How should the exercises be sequenced/intermingled?

6. If at least some structured exercises are used, how much terminology is needed? Can/should sentence combining be taught mostly by example?

Though there are no simple answers to these questions, some general observations and certain resources may help.

Francis Christensen has advocated what he calls the "cumulative" sentence, a sentence with the main subject-predicate unit followed by modifiers which are set off, usually, by commas. (The preceding sentence is an example.) As Christensen puts it, "The cumulative sentence . . . does not represent the idea as conceived, pondered over, reshaped, packaged, and delivered cold. It is dynamic rather than static, representing the mind thinking" (Christensen 1967, p. 6). As indicated in the discussion of reading, studies of children's language perception and production indicate that this cumulative sentence is in fact more natural, or at least more basic, than sentences in which the main subject and verb are interrupted by modifiers, or sentences in which the main clause is preceded by modifiers such as an adverbial clause, a participial phrase, or an absolute. Thus children just beginning sentence-combining exercises will find it easiest to create embeddings that function in the predicate part of the sentence rather than in the subject part, or that come after the main clause rather than before. Among other things, this means that we should probably have students (1) create adjectival modifiers of direct objects before creating modifiers of subjects, (2) create nominalizations to function as direct objects before creating nominalizations to function as subjects, and (3) create adverbializations which follow the main clause before creating adverbializations which come before the main clause (if, indeed, work with adverbializations seems necessary at all).

A second observation ties in with the earlier discussion of syntactic constructions that are relatively difficult to decipher. When doing sentence-combining exercises, children usually find it easier to create full relative clauses than to create the reductions of such clauses. This was illustrated in the "typical rewrites" of Hunt's sentences on aluminum: the eighth graders used several full relative clauses but only a few reductions (in particular, only a few adjectival phrases following the noun). In contrast, the twelfth graders used fewer full relative clauses but a correspondingly higher number of adjectival phrases (see pp. 39-40). It seems logical, then, to have students create full relative clauses first, and later learn to reduce such clauses in appropriate ways.

A third observation also concerns adjectival constructions. There are various kinds of adjectival constructions that might be created through sentence-combining activities, including adjectival or "relative" clauses, adjectival phrases of various sorts (including absolutes, participial phrases, prepositional phrases, appositives), and adjectival words of various sorts (including adjectives, possessives, noun adjuncts). Research seems to suggest that adjectival phrases of various sorts require the most instructional coaxing. (See also pp. 123-129.)

At the college level, I concentrate primarily on the participial phrase and the absolute. The participle is especially valuable for conveying action, while the absolute is valuable for conveying detail. The two constructions may be similar in some ways, yet they are fundamentally different. Consider the following examples:

The boy suddenly appeared in the doorway, *moving his lips unintelligibly.*	(The participial phrase focuses on the boy's *action* of moving his lips.)
The boy suddenly appeared in the doorway, *his lips moving unintelligibly.*	(The absolute phrase focuses on a *detail*, the boy's lips.)

The value of the participle and the absolute was brought home to me first by the writings of Francis Christensen (1967), and then by the ending that one of my freshmen wrote for Ray Bradbury's short story "The Foghorn." Though the student writer has shifted from one point of view to another, this ending shows considerable promise, especially for a rough draft written in twenty minutes. Later, the entire class discussed a few changes in punctuation, resulting in the version which follows:

> The monster swam faster, slicing the water with building determination; the fog horn blew, the monster exploded with a piercing scream. Swimming faster, and still faster, the monster's wake churned and foamed behind him, building higher, sucking from the depths smaller animals caught in the magnetic current. McDunn looked at Johnny: his eyes were enlarged, resembling those of the monster's, flashing red and white; his eyes bulged at the sockets, straining to see the monster.
>
> Johnny tried to speak to McDunn, yet all that broke the silence was the pulsing call of the fog horn.
>
> The monster was now fifty yards away; the eyes of the monster froze on McDunn's, locking them together. The lighthouse began to rumble; the monster was twenty yards away; the sea surged and splashed against the jagged rocks that guarded the bodyless tower. The fog horn blew in short spurts, echoing the monster's reply; the earth seemed to tremble with the monster's screams.
>
> McDunn was standing next to the window, pressing his face against the cool pane, frozen; I tried to grab him and take him to safety, but his icy arms were welded to the ledge as though steel flowed through his veins. The monster now broke through the rocks, hurling his large, beautiful shiny neck at the illuminated eye

of the lighthouse. The monster bellowed at the fog horn—McDunn
returned the thunderous scream.

McDunn and the monster faced each other, their eyes flaming,
bursting with a hateful compassionate desire. I fell into a corner,
blinded by the lighthouse light of red and white. I'm not positive,
one can't be, but it looked as though McDunn hurled himself at the
monster.

It's been eleven quiet months since that horrible night I lost
McDunn. The lighthouse is still standing. I've had to replace the
light and find a new horn; it's a curious-sounding horn, slightly
higher than the one before.

The nights seem to stretch on forever, looking at the emptiness
that isn't really empty.

After receiving this unusually fine rough draft, I began routinely
helping students learn to use the participial phrase and the absolute. In
general, students' descriptive/narrative prose has improved considerably
after only a small amount of sentence-combining practice with these two
grammatical constructions. Of course, teachers at other levels may want
to deal with other kinds of adjectival constructions as well as with the
participial phrase and the absolute. Still, my own experience suggests
that a little sentence-combining work can go a long way, at least with
older students.

Finally, there is the question of whether sentence combining should
be done apart from normal writing, in conjunction with it, or both.
First, it seems clear that sentence combining should not be done simply
as an exercise in syntactic dexterity, apart from considerations of
rhetoric. The overall quality of students' writing may even be adversely
affected if they merely engage in various kinds of sentence-combining
exercises without regard to what is effective (Mellon 1969). On the other
hand, the simultaneous consideration of grammar (what is possible) and
rhetoric (what is desirable) can have a positive overall effect on students'
writing, even when such sentence-combining activity is done apart from
the rest of the writing curriculum (O'Hare 1973). Furthermore, there is
some evidence that such sentence-combining work may have a positive
effect on reading comprehension, even when the sentence-combining
activity is done apart from the reading curriculum (Hughes 1975).

In addition, sentence combining would seem valuable during both
the prewriting and the rewriting period. This is especially true for
narrative and descriptive writing, the kinds most appropriate to the
expressive intent of the elementary school child. One of the typical
weaknesses of student writing (in *any* mode) is that it does not contain
enough specific details and/or that the details are not specific enough.
Some prewriting practice in sentence combining might help. Suppose,
for example, that the student is planning on writing a scary story about a

monster. In the prewriting stage, the student might be asked to write a general, bare-bones sentence about the monster itself, then write other sentences that further indicate the monster's appearance and actions. The student might start with something like *The monster was huge,* then add sentences like *His arms were powerful, He leaped across the river without breaking his stride, He waved his arms menacingly, His eyes were fierce with determination.* Prior practice in sentence combining and explicit guidance at this stage might encourage the student to combine these various details into a single sentence, perhaps something like the following:

> The huge monster leaped across the river without breaking his stride, waving his powerful arms menacingly, his eyes fierce with determination.

Further experimentation might lead to the placement of one modifier before the main subject-predicate unit and one after:

> Waving his powerful arms menacingly, the huge monster leaped across the river without breaking his stride, his eyes fierce with determination.

Still another possibility would be to change the modifying constructions somewhat, and to reposition them:

> Eyes fierce with determination, the huge monster leaped across the river without breaking his stride, his powerful arms waving menacingly.

Prewriting practice in creating a few such sentences should not only help the writer get the flow of language going, but should also help the writer choose details that will bring the characters, events, and setting alive for the reader.

As Francis Christensen has said, writing is essentially a process of *addition,* a process of fleshing out a grammatical skeleton, as it were, of adding details to a basic subject-predicate unit. In support of his point, Christensen quotes a passage from the writer John Erskine, a passage in which Erskine discusses "the startling gulf between the grammar which is taught and learned and the grammar which is used." Erskine discusses this gulf as follows (Christensen 1967, pp. 24-25; Erskine 1946, pp. 254-255):

> When you write, you make a point, not by subtracting as though you sharpened a pencil, but by adding. When you put one word after another, your statement should be more precise the more you add.
>
> ... the grammarian leaves with the unwary the impression that the substantive [the noun], since it can stand alone, is more

important than the adjective, that the verb is more important than the adverb, that the main clause is more important than the subordinate.

In the use of language, however, the truth is precisely the reverse. What you wish to say is found not in the noun but in what you add to qualify the noun. The noun is only a grappling iron to hitch your mind to the reader's. The noun by itself adds nothing to the reader's information; it is the name of something he knows already, and if he does not know it, you cannot do business with him. The noun, the verb, and the main clause serve merely as a base on which the meaning will rise.

The modifier is the essential part of any sentence.

These observations seem to conflict with the typical advice to avoid loading one's sentence with adjectives, and instead to pack much of one's description into strong, specific verbs. Perhaps there *is* a conflict, but it seems that Erskine is mainly arguing for the kind of sentence Christensen advocates: the cumulative sentence, with the main subject-predicate unit coming near the beginning, followed by various sorts of set-off or "free" modifiers (Christensen 1968b). Such free modifiers will inevitably be adjectival or adverbial in function, providing additional details about an entity (a noun) or about an action or condition (a verb or main clause). In the following examples, the main subject-predicate unit is italicized; every other construction is an adjectival or adverbial free modifier. The examples are from Ralph Ellison's *Invisible Man* (1952):

> *I saw the giant bend and clutch the posts at the top of the stairs with both hands,* bracing himself, his body gleaming bare in his white shorts.

> *Up ahead I saw the one who thought he was a drum major strutting in front,* giving orders as he moved energetically in long, hip-swinging strides, a cane held above his head, rising and falling as though in time to music.

> Before me, in the panel where a mirror is usually placed, *I could see a scene from a bullfight,* the bull charging close to the man and the man swinging the red cape in sculptured folds so close to his body that man and bull seemed to blend in one swirl of calm, pure motion.

Here is still another passage making generous use of free modifiers, this time a passage taken from the *New York Times* (May 5, 1970):

> *The crackle of the rifle volley cut the suddenly still air. It appeared to go on,* as a solid volley, *for perhaps a full minute or a little longer.*

> *Some of the students dived to the ground,* crawling on the grass in terror. *Others stood shocked or half crouched,* apparently believing the troops were firing into the air. *Some of the rifle barrels were pointed upward.*

> Near the top of the hill at the corner of Taylor Hall, *a student crumpled over, spun sideways and fell to the ground,* shot in the head.
>   When the firing stopped, *a slim girl,* wearing a cowboy shirt and faded jeans, *was lying face down on the road at the edge of the parking lot,* blood pouring out onto the macadam, about 10 feet from this reporter.

In the examples above, the main subject-predicate unit occurs at or near the beginning of the sentence. According to Christensen, this is characteristic of good modern prose. It is easiest and most natural for the writer to make a statement and *then* qualify or elaborate it with free modifiers. And such sentences are easiest for readers to comprehend because they can first determine the basic set of propositions represented by the main subject-predicate unit and *then* add to this set of propositions.

Such addition can doubtless be stimulated in the prewriting stage, but many students will find it easiest to add detail *after* they have written a rough draft of their work. Consequently, the rewriting period should include not merely attention to mechanics and other apparent weaknesses of the work but also to the adding of detail. Again, sentence combining may be valuable. The teacher or the writer's peers may locate two or three key sentences and help the writer explore details that could be combined into more effective, more interesting sentences. In short, it seems reasonable to do sentence combining both apart from normal writing and in conjunction with it; furthermore, sentence combining seems potentially useful in both the prewriting stage and the rewriting stage. It is not merely an exercise in syntactic dexterity, but a stimulus to vision and revision.

Selected Resources on Sentence Combining

The number of useful articles and books on sentence combining is rapidly growing, so the following list must be both idiosyncratic and incomplete. Nevertheless, these and similar materials should be of considerable value to teachers who would like to use sentence-combining activities with their students. Most of these resources do not emphasize the use of grammatical terminology and, to repeat, research indicates that formal terminology is not necessary (O'Hare 1973). The only person who needs much explicit understanding of grammar is the teacher, in order to design, select, and sequence the sentence-combining activities. And with only a little knowledge of grammar, teachers can teach sentence combining.

However, one thing must be remembered: sentence-combining activities are only an adjunct to the writing program and the writing process and should never be used as a substitute for actual writing. Sentence combining should be considered only a means, not an end in itself. With this warning, then, we suggest the following resources:

Botel, Morton, and Dawkins, John. *Communicating: The Heath English Series.* Indianapolis, Ind.: D. C. Heath & Co., 1973.
> This language arts series (grades 1-6) contains numerous sentence-combining exercises, beginning with grade 2. The exercises are usually structured by example rather than by elaborate terminology; they cover all kinds of syntactic constructions.

Christensen, Francis. *The Christensen Rhetoric Program: The Sentence and the Paragraph.* New York: Harper & Row, 1968.
> This program uses examples from literary works to help high school and college students master various kinds of free modifiers. The program includes nearly 200 overhead visuals in addition to the Student Workbook and the Teacher's Manual.

———. *Notes toward a New Rhetoric.* New York: Harper & Row, 1967.
> This pioneering collection of essays is still valuable reading for the teacher.

———. "The Problem of Defining a Mature Style." *English Journal* 57 (April 1968): 572-79.
> In effect, Christensen argues for a specific kind of sentence combining: the kind that will produce "free modifiers" in final position.

Christensen, Francis, and Christensen, Bonniejean. *A New Rhetoric.* New York: Harper & Row, 1976.
> This lucid high school/college text is divided into two major sections. The first concentrates on the sentence and especially on the free modifier, while the second emphasizes the paragraph and larger units of composition.

Cooper, Charles R. "An Outline for Writing Sentence-Combining Problems." *English Journal* 62 (1973): 96-102, 108.
> Illustrates different kinds of sentence-combining exercises, according to syntactic structure and transformation. The exercises are structured, and the emphasis is on relatively sophisticated kinds of constructions.

Gibson, Walker. *Persona: A Style Study for Readers and Writers.* New York: Random House, 1969.
> In this interesting little high school/college text, Gibson discusses various aspects of style, with some attention to sentence structure.

Gould, Victor E. *Experiments in Effective Writing.* New York: Harcourt Brace Jovanovich, 1972.
> Drawing upon the work of Christensen and others, this high school text provides practice with a variety of syntactic constructions.

Klarner, Walter E.; Williams, James M.; and Harp, Harold L. *Writing by Design.* Boston: Houghton Mifflin Co., 1977.
> This college text draws heavily upon Christensen's work in helping students write description, narration, exposition, and argument.

Martin, Bill Jr., and Brogan, Peggy. *Teaching Suggestions for 'Sounds Jubilee'*
and 'Sounds Freedomring.' New York: Holt, Rinehart & Winston, 1975, 1972.
Though not explicitly involving sentence combining, many of the
suggested activities involve various kinds of syntactic manipulation.

Ney, James W. "Notes towards a Psycholinguistic Model of the Writing Process."
Research in the Teaching of English 8 (1974): 157-69.
Drawing upon his work with fourth graders, Ney discusses develop-
mental trends in sentence-combining ability.

O'Hare, Frank. *Sentence Combining: Improving Student Writing without*
Formal Grammar Instruction. Research Report No. 15. Urbana, Ill.: National
Council of Teachers of English, 1973.
Appendix A and Appendix B contain 21 pages of the structured
sentence-combining exercises O'Hare used with the seventh graders
in this experiment. O'Hare's research is highly significant, and the
review of previous research and the discussion of O'Hare's own
research are well worth reading.

_____. *Sentencecraft.* Lexington, Mass.: Ginn & Co., 1975.
High school text, with each unit of sentence-combining exercises
followed by "writing workshops" with elective topics for writing
assignments.

Perron, Jack. "Beginning Writing: It's All in the Mind." *Language Arts* 53 (1976):
652-57.
Perron describes a variety of sentence-combining games, exercises,
and experiential activities that he used successfully with fourth
graders.

Strong, William. *Sentence Combining.* New York: Random House, 1973.
Highly useful book of exercises, for seventh grade (approximately)
through adult. Most of the exercises are unstructured.

_____. "Sentence-Combining: Back to Basics and Beyond." *English Journal* 65
(1976): 56, 60-64.
Presents a rationale for sentence combining, plus practical suggestions for incorporating sentence combining into the curriculum.

Summary

Standardized tests of mechanics should not be used to evaluate student
writing because (1) the use of such tests perpetuates the hypothesis that
writing means producing written language that is superficially "correct,"
(2) such tests tend to discriminate against those who speak a nonstandard dialect, (3) such tests measure little more than *one* broad aspect of
writing, namely mechanics, and (4) there may be little correlation
between scores on such a test and actual writing ability. Instead of using
standardized tests to evaluate writing, there should be a multi-
dimensional program which evaluates various aspects of actual student

writing. Such a program should acknowledge the fact that young writers progress only gradually from expressive to transactional and poetic writing; should take into account what children meant to say or tried to do, as well as what they actually did; should evaluate and reward errors which are a sign of progress; and should evaluate the student's writing according to specified criteria and/or according to the student's progress, rather than in comparison with some kind of average or "norm."

Concerning mechanics, it has long been maintained that a knowledge of grammar can improve such mechanical aspects of writing as punctuation, sentence structure, and usage. Attention to mechanics is most appropriate in the *rewriting* stage, when the writer is most able to attend to the needs and demands of an audience. However, prior knowledge of grammar is much less useful to the student than direct assistance from the teacher or even from peers. Furthermore, teachers must avoid trying to get students to "correct" all the mechanical faults of their writing at once. Instead, teachers should generally concentrate on no more than one or two details of mechanics for any given paper. Direct classroom instruction in mechanics should be used sparingly, since its positive effect is usually negligible. Such instruction is most likely to succeed when it meets a felt need on the part of students, when it covers neither too many aspects of mechanics nor too few, and when it deals with real writing rather than with textbook exercises. Even then, however, it is not necessary for students to have prior knowledge of grammatical terminology; teachers can simply introduce a minimum of terminology as it is needed, teaching more by example than by explanation.

In short, grammatical knowledge is more useful to teachers than to students. Teachers with some explicit knowledge of grammar should be able to design, select, and sequence a variety of sentence-combining activities. Students who have had considerable amount of practice with such activities tend to show improved control of sentence structure in their free writing, an increased ability to write syntactically mature sentences. There is some evidence that such practice may also improve reading comprehension. But before incorporating such exercises into the English language arts curriculum, teachers need to make such decisions as (1) which kinds of exercises are appropriate for the students' level of development; (2) whether such exercises should cover a variety of syntactic constructions or only a few; (3) whether the sentence combining should be done apart from normal writing, in conjunction with it, or both; (4) whether such exercises should be written or oral or both; (5) whether such exercises should be structured, unstructured, or both; (6) and whether to use technical terminology in the exercises or whether to teach mainly by example.

One important point is that grammar needs to be combined with rhetoric; that is, students need not only to practice ways of combining sentences but to discuss which ways are more effective and why. Practice in creating cumulative sentences should be especially beneficial: the writer makes a statement in the main subject-predicate unit, then adds free modifiers. Such modifiers enable a writer to provide additional details about an entity (a noun) or about an action or condition (a verb or main clause) without giving these details the same rhetorical weight as the main statement. Another advantage of sentence combining in general and the cumulative sentence in particular is that it seems to stimulate thought. Attention to *how to say* helps writers decide *what to say*. Thus, although sentence combining must *not* replace practice in actual writing, it can help students explore the possibilities of their subject before beginning to write, and it can help them add effective detail after they have written a rough draft. In short, teachers can use their own knowledge of grammar to help students combine syntactic maturity with depth of vision, to help students use detail with the skill of a professional.

5 What to Do with Grammar

Now we return to the basic question: Should grammar be a formal part of the English language arts curriculum? As indicated earlier, one valid reason for teaching grammar may simply be that language is such a marvelous human achievement it deserves to be studied. Another reason may be that, properly approached, the study of grammar can help students discover how to collect data, formulate and test hypotheses, draw generalizations—in short, it can help students learn to approach something as the scientist does. However, the most common reason for teaching grammar has been the assumption that it will have a positive effect upon students' ability to use the language.

Unfortunately, this assumption seems unwarranted. As long ago as 1950, the *Encyclopedia of Educational Research* indicated that certain pessimistic statements concerning the formal teaching of grammar seemed to be supported by "the best opinion, practice, and experimental evidence." These statements are as follows (p. 393):

1. The disciplinary value which may be attributed to formal grammar is negligible.

2. No more relation exists between knowledge of grammar and the application of the knowledge in a functional language situation than exists between any two totally different and unrelated school subjects.

3. In spite of the fact that the contribution of the knowledge of English grammar to achievement in foreign language has been its chief justification in the past, the experimental evidence does not support this conclusion.

4. The study of grammar has been justified because of its possible contribution to reading skills, but the evidence does not support this conclusion.

5. The contribution of grammar to the formation of sentences in speech and in writing has doubtless been exaggerated.

6. Grammar is difficult if not impossible to teach to the point of practical application.

7. Formal and traditional grammar contains many items which if learned to the point of application could not have any serious effect on the learner's language usage.

8. Many grammatical rules have been stated which have little or no basis in acceptable speech and writing.

9. Much of grammar based upon analogy, history, logic, or an ideally perfect language may be disregarded. The only valid grammatical generalizations must be based upon acceptable language practices. Current usage furnishes the only legitimate standards.

Many modern handbooks of grammar have weeded out some of the "rules" which have no basis in current educated usage, but otherwise the situation remains much the same as in 1950: there is little evidence that the formal study of grammar has much of a positive effect on students' use of language (see for example Elley et al. 1975, Petrosky's 1977 review, and the SLATE 1976 Starter Sheets on "Back to the Basics"). Studies which at first seemed to prove the value of grammar study have generally not seemed so conclusive, upon careful reexamination.

Take, for example, the early study by Bateman and Zidonis (1966), who were perhaps the first researchers to investigate the effect that studying transformational grammar might have upon students' writing. Their experimental group showed fewer sentence structure errors than the control group, and at the same time the experimental group used more mature sentence structures. However, the increase in syntactic maturity may be due to the students' practice in sentence combining rather than to their study of transformational grammar per se. And indeed, O'Hare has found that sentence combining can produce the same kind of results, without the formal study of grammar or the use of technical terminology (O'Hare 1973).

In short, then, DeBoer's earlier summary still seems appropriate (1959, p. 417):

> The impressive fact is... that in all these studies, carried out in places and at times far removed from each other, often by highly experienced and disinterested investigators, the results have been consistently negative so far as the value of grammar in the improvement of language expression is concerned. Surely there is no justification in the available evidence for the great expenditure of time and effort still being devoted to formal grammar in American schools.

Indeed, formal instruction in grammar may have a harmful effect, partly because it tends to alienate students, and partly because it takes time that might more profitably be used in helping students read, write, listen, and speak more effectively.

Let us be clear, however, on what we mean. There is little pragmatic justification for systematically teaching a grammar of the language, whether that grammar be traditional, structural, transformational, or whatever. On the other hand, it may be desirable or even necessary to use some grammatical concepts and terminology in helping students become more effective language users. Thus the *teacher* needs a fairly solid background in grammar in order to work with students.

With some explicit knowledge of grammar, teachers are better prepared to help students avoid or correct certain kinds of problems with sentence structure, punctuation, and usage. Take, for example, the semicolon, which is most commonly used to join two T-units (see pp. 145-146). In order to help students understand this use, Gliserman made up a set of rules for a poem (1978, p. 798):

> Animal$_1$ + present action verb + color + complement;
> Animal$_2$ + present action verb + color + complement.

Here are some of the lines his students created in response to this formula:

> Elephants run blue skies; tigers walk black ground.
> Cows sing blue notes; horses play green guitars.
> Bears dream blue dreams; birds sleep green feathers.
> Grasshoppers jump high above the green grass; ants crawl along the rich brown earth.

Gliserman's *However* poem reinforces not only the use of the semicolon, but also the use of the conjunctive adverb *however* (p. 799):

> Form: Structure$_1$ is made of *something*; however, Structure$_2$ is made of *something else.*
> Example: Shacks are made of wet feathers; however, gas stations are made of toothpicks.

Although work with the semicolon is appropriate mainly for older students, it should be relatively easy to design similar "grammar poems" for younger students as well. Many of the formats suggested in Kenneth Koch's *Wishes, Lies, and Dreams* (Random House, 1970) could be modified to emphasize grammar and punctuation as well as content.

Another interesting and profitable topic is multiple negation in modern English. Instead of merely issuing an edict against double negatives and red-inking the students' margins, we might open-mindedly examine the role of double and multiple negatives in today's speech and writing. As a starter, see what happens when you try to make the following sentences negative:

> I want some.
> He found some candy.
> He should be going somewhere.
> I can do something about it.

Most of us tend not only to add a negative *not* or *n't* (plus auxiliary, if necessary), but also to change *some* to *any*:

> I don't want *any*.
> He did*n't* find *any* candy.
> He should*n't* be going *anywhere*.
> I ca*n't* do *any*thing about it.

In short, when a positive sentence contains an indefinite *some*, we add not one negative marker but two. Both standard and nonstandard English have "double" negatives in such cases; they simply differ in the specific indefinite negative, *any* versus *none* or *no*:

Standard English	Nonstandard English
I don't want *any*.	I don't want *none*.
He didn't find *any* candy.	He didn't find *no* candy.
He shouldn't be going *anywhere*.	He shouldn't be going *nowhere*.
I can't do *anything* about it.	I can't do *nothing* about it.

To further explore the notion that there are different kinds of double negatives, teachers might try the similar exercise in Rutherford (1973, p. 47), or an exercise something like the following:

> Do two negatives make a positive in the following sentences?
>
> That's not illogical.
> That's not impossible.
> He's not dishonest.
> That's not a disinfectant.
> He ain't got no money.
> She didn't go nowhere.
> You can't do it neither.

The first four of these sentences usually provoke lively discussion, since they seem to express neither a negative nor a full-fledged positive, but a rather lukewarm positive.

Additional work with multiple negatives might focus on developing rules which describe how the following kinds of negatives are formed from the underlying positive statements:

	Positive	Negative
Type 1	I want some.	I don't want none.
	He should be going somewhere.	He shouldn't be going nowhere.
Type 2	Something can happen.	Nothing can't happen.
	Somebody is coming.	Nobody ain't coming.

Type 3	Something can happen.	Can't nothing happen.
	Somebody is coming.	Ain't nobody coming.
	There is something you can do.	Ain't nothing you can do.

It may help both teachers and students to see that nonstandard negatives are just as rule-governed as "standard" negatives; the rules are simply different (see Burling 1973 for a fuller treatment). Acknowledging this fact should make it easier for teachers to get students to use the so-called standard forms when appropriate.

The suggested grammar poems are themselves a writing activity of sorts, and certainly the exploration of negation does not need to be tied to any particular writing assignment. However, certain kinds of activities may work best in the rewriting phase when they meet a demonstrated need.

Chaika (1978) and Gliserman (1978) suggest useful activities for helping students understand and avoid such perennial problems as the dangling modifier, the fragment, and the run-on (comma splice). The explanations in traditional grammar handbooks are often unclear and unhelpful, as Chaika points out. She cites, for example, the *Harbrace College Handbook*'s definition of a *dangling* construction (Harcourt Brace Jovanovich, 1972, p. 277; p. 776 in Chaika):

> a construction that hangs loosely within a sentence; the term *dangling* is applied primarily to incoherent verbal phrases and elliptical clauses. A dangling modifier is one that does not refer clearly and logically to some word in the sentence.

Unfortunately, this definition is both unclear and untruthful. A dangling modifier is usually clear to both the writer and the reader; it simply does not conform to the "rule" that in formal written English, the underlying subject of such a construction must be the same as the subject of the main clause. As an example, let us take this sentence:

> Standing on the corner, trains rush by every hour.

To most of us, that sentence would be perfectly clear: when you're standing on the corner, you see trains rushing by every hour (or something similar). The problem is not really one of clarity, but one of convention. The underlying subjects of both parts are supposed to be the same, but they are not.

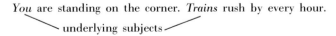

You are standing on the corner. *Trains* rush by every hour.

In writing formal English, the student should either avoid the participle altogether, or reconstruct the sentence so that the underlying subjects are the same:

Standing on the corner, you see trains rushing by every hour.

This version is still relatively informal because of the "you"; however, it does reflect the rule that the underlying subject of such a construction must be the same as the subject of the main clause. Note that this explanation is probably clearer than the more traditional explanation that the participle must "modify" the subject of the main clause. It usually helps to emphasize the underlying sentences and the *processes* involved in going from deep structure to surface structure. For this reason, many such grammar rules are best taught through sentence-combining activities, then reviewed as necessary.

To deal with such problems in the rewriting stage, Gliserman suggests that teachers have a set of self-teaching worksheets on various aspects of sentence structure, punctuation, and usage. He suggests the following kind of worksheet for learning to identify and eliminate sentence fragments (his format, my examples):

> *Problem 1.* Note that a sentence can often be turned into a variety of grammatical fragments. For example, *He jogs every morning* can be turned into such fragments as:
>
> jogging every morning
> that he jogs every morning
> since he jogs every morning
> for him to jog every morning
>
> Similarly, take each sentence in the following list and turn it into a variety of grammatical fragments:
>
> 1. Elaine wins the race every year.
> 2. You ski in Colorado.
> 3. Marvin will quit now.
> 4. They stole the money.
>
> *Problem 2.* Take the fragments that you have just made and add whatever elements are needed to make them into complete sentences. For example, the "jogging" fragments could be made into complete sentences as follows:
>
> Jogging every morning takes a lot of will power.
> Did you know that he jogs every morning?
> He should be healthy, since he jogs every morning.
> It would be good for him to jog every morning.
>
> *Problem 3.* Some of the following strings of words are grammatical fragments and some are complete sentences. Pick out the fragments and use them so that they become complete sentences:

1. Being a good athlete.
2. Flying to California on a 747.
3. When Marcie left.
4. Being taller than Bob, she got the cookie jar.
5. Because they were hungry.
6. He is escaping from school.
7. That they were lonely.

Note that the emphasis here is again on process and on the active involvement of the student. While such a worksheet might not be as effective as a brief conference with the teacher or with a peer who serves as "editor," at least it can be reserved for those who actually have trouble with sentence fragments. Individualized instruction on selected aspects of grammar and writing is vastly different from the formal teaching of grammar to an entire class.

An understanding of grammar can be useful, too, in helping students understand and appreciate literature. Think, for example, of some of the problems encountered in reading Shakespeare. Vocabulary is certainly one of the difficulties, but so is syntax. Some of these syntactic difficulties might be forestalled through prereading activities like those suggested by Katz (1971). The following exercises are just a few that could be used to help students with the syntax of Shakespeare (Malmstrom and Weaver 1973, pp. 111, 118, and 125). The examples are from *Romeo and Juliet*:

1. Make the following negatives into their present-day equivalents. Judging from these examples, how were Middle English affirmative sentences negated when there was no auxiliary verb? How are such sentences negated now?

   Venus smiles not in a house of tears (IV.i.8)

   he speaks not true (III.i.175)

   Therefore he that cannot lick his fingers/ goes not with me (IV.ii.7-8)

   you know/ not how to choose a man (II.v.38-39)

   You know not what you do (I.i.62)

   I would [wish] I knew not why it should be slowed (IV.i.16)

2. Make the following questions into their present-day equivalents. Judging from these examples, how were Middle English declarative sentences made into yes/no questions and WH-questions when there was no auxiliary verb? How are such sentences made into questions now?

   Saw you him to-day? (I.i.114)

   Need you my help? (IV.iii.6)

And weep ye now... ? (IV.v.73)

How stands your disposition to be married? (I.iii.65)

wherefore weep I then? (III.ii.107)

Why call you for a sword? (I.i.74)

What say you? (I.iii.79)

Whence come you? (III.iii.78)

3. Make the following sentences into their Middle English equivalents:

Do you have enough time?
Did he leave yesterday?
What does he think?
Why didn't she stay?

Such activities can provide an interesting challenge as well as ultimately help students cope with Shakespeare.

Other activities can move from the study of literature to the students' own experiments with effective style. Consider, for example, the two passages below. One is the original, from James Baldwin's *Nobody Knows My Name* (pp. 28-29). The other is a rewrite by Jacobs and Rosenbaum (1971, p. 39). The two versions differ primarily in the use of the WHAT-cleft transformation:

And yet, that there *was* something which all black men held in common became clear as the debate wore on. They held in common their precarious, their unutterably painful relation to the white world. They held in common the necessity to remake the world in their own image, to impose this image on the world.... The vision of the world, and of themselves which other people held would no longer control them. In sum, black men held in common their ache to come into the world as men.

And yet, it became clear as the debate wore on, that there *was* something which all black men held in common.... What they held in common was their precarious, their unutterably painful relation to the white world. What they held in common was the necessity to remake the world in their own image, to impose this image on the world, and no longer be controlled by the vision of the world, and of themselves, held by other people. What, in sum, black men held in common was their ache to come into the world as men.

After students have discussed which version is more effective and why, they can be asked to experiment with the effects of different "stylistic transformations" in their own writing (see pp. 139-142).

Postman and Weingartner, for example, provide interesting activities in which students explore the uses of the passive voice (1966, pp. 118-119):

Problem 1

Following is the opening paragraph of a short story, "The Great Wall of China," by Franz Kafka. Read it carefully.

The Great Wall of China was finished off at its northernmost corner. From the south-east and the south-west it came up in two sections that finally converged there. This principle of piecemeal construction was also applied on a smaller scale by both of the two great armies of labor, the eastern and the western. It was done in this way: gangs of some twenty workers were formed who had to accomplish a length, say, of five hundred yards of wall, while a similar gang built another stretch of the same length to meet the first. But after the junction had been made the construction of the wall was not carried on from the point, let us say, where this thousand yards ended; instead the two groups of workers were transferred to begin building again in quite different neighborhoods. Naturally in this way many great gaps were left, which were only filled in gradually and bit by bit, some, indeed, not till after the official announcement that the wall was finished. In fact it is said that there are gaps which have never been filled in at all, an assertion, however, which is probably merely one more of the many legends to which the building of the wall gave rise, and which cannot be verified, at least by any single man with his own eyes and judgment, on account of the extent of the structure.

Answer the following questions:

1. Who "finished off" the Great Wall of China? How far must you read until you can answer?
2. Who directed the formation of the gangs of workers? Do you know?
3. Who was in command of the building of the wall? Do you know?
4. Who transferred the groups of workers to different locations? Do you know?
5. Does the narrator think the wall itself, the people building it, or the people directing its construction are more important? How do you know?
6. Can you relate your answers to Questions 1 to 5 to the sentence structure of the paragraph?

Problem 2

In your notebook, list all the verbs in the paragraph you have just read. Then, rewrite the paragraph, changing the structure of the sentences so that all the verbs are in the active voice. Your paragraph might begin:

The two great armies of labor finished off the Great Wall of China at its northernmost corner.

Problem 3

Compare your version of the paragraph with the original by answering the following questions:

1. How do the purposes of the two versions differ?
2. How does the tone of your version differ from that of the original?
3. Is there a difference in emphasis between your version and the original? Explain.

Again, such activities only begin to indicate the ways in which teachers can put their own knowledge of grammar to use.

Given, then, that grammar is useful for teachers, Part Two provides an introduction to English grammar and grammatical theories. But English language arts teachers need more than just a knowledge of grammar. They need to have a general interest in and excitement about language and its possibilities, an understanding of the language processes, and a respect for students' intuitive grasp of language structure. Such teachers will not dose their students with grammar, but rather engage students in using their language resources and expanding their ability to comprehend and use language well.

II Grammar as Product, Process, and Guidebook

This part of the book presents a brief description of some of the essentials of English grammar. Although the language arts teacher or English teacher may never teach grammar systematically, it is important for teachers to understand both the structure of already formed sentences and the processes by which sentences may be formed, as well as the common "rules" for sentence construction and punctuation in formal written English. With such an understanding, teachers are better prepared to assess the abilities and meet the needs of readers and writers.

Nowadays, most teachers are acquainted with at least the names of the three kinds of grammar that have recently been described in textbooks: *traditional*, *structural*, and *transformational*. These grammars will be compared in the following section. This comparison will be followed by three sections presenting specifics of English grammar: English Grammar as Product, English Grammar as Process, and English Grammar as Guidebook. The first of these three sections reflects mainly a traditional and structural orientation; the second reflects a transformational orientation; and the third section draws upon all three grammatical orientations while illustrating the aims of traditional school grammars.

6 Comparing Grammars

Traditional school grammars have their roots in medieval scholarship and medieval society. "Grammar" was then thought to be a reflection of logic. Even as late as the nineteenth century one finds an occasional statement like that of John Stuart Mill:

> Consider for a moment what grammar is. It is the most elementary part of logic. It is the beginning of the analysis of the thinking process. The principles and rules of grammar are the means by which the forms of language are made to correspond with the universal forms of thought.[19]

Small wonder, then, that in Britain the traditional term for "secondary school" was for a long time "grammar school."

Until the eighteenth century, however, "grammar" was more or less synonymous with "Latin grammar." Latin was thought to be the most logical language, the most accurate reflection of thought; other languages were "degenerate" and not worthy of description or study. When at last scholars did turn to the analysis and description of such languages as English, they naturally used Latin categories and terms for their descriptions. Since Latin had many more word endings than English, this procedure led to an overabundance of terms in describing the English language (as well as inappropriate rules for its proper use). Naturally, the terms were often based upon meaning, since grammar was considered a reflection of thought. A good example is the traditional schoolbook definition of a sentence: "a sentence is a group of words expressing a complete thought."

During the Middle Ages and even later, Latin was a means to social advancement: "One had to learn not only to read Latin, but also to write Latin, if one wanted to maintain no matter how humble a position in the republic of learning or in the hierarchy of the church." Thus the study of "grammar" was chiefly a study of how to write Latin correctly. "This you must say, and these faults you must avoid—such were the lessons imparted in the schools. Grammar was not a set of facts observed but of rules to be observed. . . . In other words, grammar was *prescriptive* rather than *descriptive*" (Jespersen 1922, p. 24). This prescriptive tradition carried over into traditional school grammars of English, reinforced by the social needs of newly rich English during the Industrial Revolution and the similar needs of newly arrived and newly rich Americans. The purpose of the traditional school grammar book has long been to help people master a socially prestigious form of the language.[20] Along with the dictionary, it is a *guidebook* or etiquette book, the Emily Post of the language. A longtime favorite is John Warriner's *English Grammar and Composition Series* (1959; last revised, 1977). For teachers, an up-to-date guide to current educated usage, grammar, and related matters is *Index to English*, by Wilma R. Ebbitt and David R. Ebbitt (6th ed., 1977).

Traditional scholarly grammars derive from a far different tradition. While engaged in the historical and comparative study of languages, various nineteenth century scholars collected a vast amount of data concerning English. From this data, they wrote grammars in which they tried to describe the language as it is actually used, rather than as people think it ought to be used. They sought to describe the *product*, to base their grammars on direct observations of speech. These efforts resulted in impressive descriptive grammars, well exemplified by Otto Jespersen's *Essentials of English Grammar* (1933). Such grammars usually reflect an attempt to relate meaning to form and function whenever possible. An example is Jespersen's definition of a sentence: "A sentence is a (relatively) complete and independent unit of communication (or—in the case of soliloquy—what might be a communication were there someone to listen to it)—the completeness and independence being shown by its standing alone or its capability of standing alone, *i.e.* of being uttered by itself" (Jespersen 1933, p. 106). Here, Jespersen draws a connection between completeness of thought and independence of form.

The grammars of *structural linguists* are in some ways similar to those of the traditional scholarly grammarians, but in other ways different. Structural linguistics grew out of anthropological linguistics in the 1920s and 1930s, when scholars were avidly seeking to describe American Indian languages. Such linguists insisted on approaching each language without preconceptions as to its structure; they sought to write grammars that would *describe* the language accurately. In like manner, the structuralists of the 1950s sought to describe English as it was actually spoken, the *product*, without prior notions of its elements or structure. This sometimes resulted in rather unusual-looking grammars, where the traditional "noun" and "verb" were described as "Form class 1" and "Form class 2" respectively; an example is Charles Fries's *The Structure of English* (1952). Thus the structuralists were like the traditional scholarly grammarians in their concern to describe English as it is actually used. They differed, however, in a significant aspect of their method.

Unlike the traditionalists, the structuralists objected to defining grammatical terms by appealing to meaning. One reason was simply that such definitions are unhelpful: defining a sentence as "a group of words expressing a complete thought" doesn't help people distinguish sentences from nonsentences; one needs more precise definitions and/or a wide range of examples. In the structuralists' opinion, a basic problem was that "meaning" and "thought" are imprecise terms. Leonard Bloomfield, the father of structural linguistics, wrote in 1933: "The statement of meanings is ... the weak point in language study, and will remain so until human knowledge advances very far beyond its present state" (p. 140). Thus the structuralists ignored meaning as much as possible in writing their descriptive grammars of English. Bloomfield's definition of the sentence is typical: "Each sentence is an independent linguistic form, not included by virtue of any grammatical construction in any larger linguistic form" (Bloomfield 1933, p. 170). Here there is no appeal to thought or to meaning, only to form (though one may well object that the term "form" is as nebulous in this definition as the term "thought" in the traditional schoolbook definition). For high school use, a fine structural grammar text is Paul Roberts's *Patterns of English* (1956).

Beginning in 1957 with Noam Chomsky, the transformationalists took issue with the structuralists' insistence upon ignoring meaning in their grammatical descriptions. One reason was simply that grammatical function is often impossible to describe in any significant way, or even to determine, without referring to meaning. Compare, for example, the sentences *Snoopy is eager to see* and *Snoopy is easy to see*. In the first case, Snoopy is the one who sees; in the second case, Snoopy is the one who is seen. How do we know this? Simply by knowing that people and animals may be described as "eager," but actions may not; and that actions may be described as "easy," but people or animals usually are not (except in the sexual sense: "She is easy"). In order to fully understand the structure of the example sentences, we must understand their meaning.

Transformationalists seldom concern themselves with defining terms like "sentence"; instead, they simply try to describe our intuitive knowledge about how the language is structured, our unconscious "sentence sense." In Chomsky's view, this is one of the primary functions of a grammar: to describe a native speaker's unconscious knowledge of what is and what is not grammatical in the language. A grammar should describe not merely human speech, but the language system which underlies acts of speech. Thus Chomsky postulated two levels of language structure, a *surface* level and a *deep* level. Updating his explanation somewhat, we might say that the surface level consists of a linear sequence of clauses, phrases, words, and sounds or letters. The deep level consists of the underlying propositions and the relationships among them. Thus underlying the surface *Snoopy is easy to see* is a deep structure which shows the appropriate relationship between the proposition "Someone can see Snoopy" and the proposition "Something is easy." Or to put it more generally, a *sentence* might be defined as a linear sequence of linguistic units (a surface structure) which reflects one or more underlying propositions and relations (a deep structure). The surface structure is the form, while the deep structure indicates at least certain aspects of the meaning.

The transformationalists have insisted that their process grammars cannot hope to be an accurate reflection of how people actually produce or perceive sentences. Nevertheless, Chomsky himself has predicted that "the major contribution of the study of language will lie in the understanding it can provide as to the character of mental processes and the structures they form and manipulate" (Chomsky 1968, p. 59).

A fine transformational grammar for junior high or high school is Jean Malmstrom's *Grammar Basics: A Reading/Writing Approach* (1977).

Summary

Traditional scholarly grammarians were concerned with describing both the surface level and the deep level of language structure, and they were interested in the relationships between the two levels. In contrast, the structuralists were concerned with describing only the surface level. The transformationalists and their intellectual descendants have come full circle, back to the concern of the traditional scholarly grammarians, but with a new twist: the transformationalists have been concerned primarily with the *processes* by which deep structure is *transformed* into surface structure. Hence the name *transformational* grammar.

7 Grammar as Product

This section will occasionally reflect the insights of transformational grammarians, but will draw more heavily upon traditional grammar (with its emphasis on meaning) and upon structural grammar (with its emphasis on form and function). Traditional grammar is important, if only because its terminology is widely known and because its appeal to meaning is often vital in determining the precise function of a grammatical unit. Structural grammar is important because it lends precision to definitions and to procedures for identifying grammatical units and their functions.

The description will be primarily concerned with *content words* (nouns, verbs, adjectives, and adverbs) and only secondarily concerned with the *function words* that stand for content words or glue them together into a surface structure (mainly pronouns, noun determiners, verb auxiliaries, conjunctive adverbs, coordinating conjunctions, and subordinating conjunctions).

Content words can usually be identified by their *form* and/or their *function*. There are two kinds of endings by which these major parts of speech may often be identified: *inflectional* and *derivational*. Roughly speaking, an inflectional ending is one added to a word as it joins with other words in a sentence. Since there are just a few inflectional endings, these will all be presented. The class of derivational endings is much larger, consisting of all those that are not inflectional; many of these endings "derive" one part of speech from another. Some common derivational endings will be presented for each major part of speech. In addition to these forms by which the parts of speech may be identified, there are characteristic functions; these too will be discussed.

Nouns, Pronouns, and Noun Determiners

Nouns

A *noun* is traditionally defined as a word that names a person, place, thing, or idea. Structurally, a noun may be defined as any word that takes a noun ending. There are two kinds of inflectional endings by

105

which many nouns may be identified: *plural* (as in *bobcats*) and/or *possessive* (as in *bobcat's* and *bobcats'*; the latter example indicates both plural and possessive). In addition, there are several derivational endings by which some nouns may be identified. The following words illustrate some common derivational endings for nouns: *conveyance, claimant, absence, consistency, employee, baker, communism, physicist, community, agreement, happiness*. Note that *-er* is also an adjective ending (e.g. *hotter*) and sometimes an adjective or adverb ending (e.g. *slower*).

Nouns have five basic functions: subject of a clause, direct object of a verb, predicate nominative, object of a preposition, and indirect object of a verb.

1.   *Subject of a clause.* A *clause* is traditionally said to consist of a noun (someone or something) about which something is predicated. These two basic parts of the clause are the *subject* and the *predicate*, respectively. Thus the most basic function of a noun is to serve as the subject of a clause: *Ebenezer* snores, *Ebenezer* is king, *Ebenezer* eats peanuts.

2.   *Direct object of a verb.* A direct object is a noun that occurs after the verb and that is traditionally said to "receive the action of the verb." A direct object ordinarily refers to a *different* real world entity than the subject does: Ebenezer eats *peanuts*, Ebenezer knows *arithmetic*.

3.   *Predicate nominative.* A predicate nominative is a noun that occurs after the verb (i.e. in the predicate part of the sentence) and that refers to the *same* real world entity as the subject: Ebenezer is *king*, Ebenezer became *king*.

4.   *Object of a preposition.* Another way a noun can function is as the object of a preposition; together, the preposition and the following noun constitute a *prepositional phrase*. The following words are those which most commonly function as prepositions: *at, by, for, from, in, of, on, to,* and *with*. Prepositional phrases can be illustrated as follows: John stared *at Ebenezer*, John stood *by Ebenezer*, John played *with Ebenezer*. In each case the noun "Ebenezer" is the object of the preposition.

The following is a more complete list of words which *can* function as prepositions, though some of them may have other functions as well:

about	around	besides	for
above	as	between	from
across	at	beyond	in
after	before	by	into
against	behind	concerning	like
along	below	down	near
amid	beneath	during	of
among	beside	except	off

on	since	toward	up
onto	through	under	upon
out	throughout	underneath	with
over	till	until	within
past	to	unto	without

5. *Indirect object of a verb.* Another way a noun can function is as the indirect object of a verb. The indirect object always comes before a direct object and indicates the one to whom or for whom something is given, said, or done: John gave *Ebenezer* peanuts, John bought *Ebenezer* peanuts. An indirect object can always be paraphrased by a prepositional phrase introduced by *to* or *for*, as in: John gave peanuts to Ebenezer; John bought peanuts for Ebenezer.

In summary, then, we can define a *noun* as any word which takes a noun ending. Any word or construction that functions like a noun can be called a *nominal*. A nominal can consist of a word, a phrase, a near-clause, or a clause. A *phrase* has a *head word* which is ordinarily described or "modified" by everything else (in this case, a head *noun*).[21] A *clause* has no head word, but rather a subject-plus-predicate structure. A *near-clause* shows evidence of an underlying subject-plus-verb unit, even though it does not have the normal structure of a clause. The various kinds of nominals may be illustrated as follows:

Word: Ebenezer eats *peanuts.* John likes *him.*

Phrase: Ebenezer eats *the old, wrinkly peanuts that John brings him.*

              (head noun)

Near-clause: Ebenezer likes *John's bringing him peanuts.*

              Ebenezer likes *for John to bring him peanuts.*

              (In these cases, *John* is the underlying subject and *bring* is the underlying verb.)

Clause: Ebenezer thinks *that John will bring him peanuts.*

              (subject)   (predicate)

              Ebenezer likes *whoever brings him peanuts.*

              (subject)   (predicate)

Note that we can identify these constructions as nominals because each can be replaced with the word *something* or the word *someone*. For convenience, nominals have been illustrated as direct objects only. However, each kind of nominal can be used in any of the five basic noun functions: subject, direct object, predicate nominative, object of a preposition, and indirect object.

Pronouns

We turn now to pronouns. Traditionally, a *pronoun* is defined as a word used in place of a noun. Unfortunately, however, the matter is not so simple: there are several kinds of pronouns, and these have varying functions. Here, we will discuss three kinds: *indefinite pronouns*, *demonstrative pronouns*, and *personal pronouns*.

 1. Indefinite pronouns. Some of the most common indefinite pronouns are:

anyone	everybody	no one	someone
anybody	everyone	nobody	somebody
anything	everything	nothing	something

These do indeed function as nouns:

>Ebenezer doesn't need *anything.*
>*Everyone* can go.
>*Nothing* happened.
>Ebenezer saw *somebody.*

However, other so-called indefinite pronouns may function either as a noun or as a *noun determiner*, to signal that a noun will follow, although not necessarily as the next word:[22]

all	either	much
another	few	neither
any	many	other
both	more	several
each	most	some
no (determiner)		none (noun)

Here are some examples of both uses:

Noun	Noun determiner
Ebenezer doesn't want *any.*	Ebenezer doesn't want *any* peanuts.
Most like peanuts.	*Most* elephants like peanuts.
John doesn't want *much.*	John doesn't want *much* applesauce.
John wants *some.*	John wants *some* peanuts.
None likes candy.	*No* elephant likes candy.

Although the italicized words in the left column are technically functioning as nouns, we mentally interpret them as noun determiners, with the noun understood from context (or not understood at all, as the case may be).

2. Demonstrative Pronouns. The so-called demonstrative pronouns are as follows:

Singular	Plural
this	these
that	those

Again, however, these are words which can function either as a *noun* or as a *noun determiner*:

Noun	Noun determiner
Ebenezer likes *these*.	Ebenezer likes *these* peanuts.
Ebenezer doesn't like *that*.	Ebenezer doesn't like *that* candy.

3. Personal Pronouns. With the so-called personal pronouns, the situation is more complex: most forms function as nouns, but the so-called "first possessive" forms function as noun determiners.

Before listing the personal pronoun forms, it would be well to define some terms. *First person* refers to the speaker; *second person* refers to the person or persons spoken to; *third person* refers to the person or persons spoken about. For example:

I'm telling *you*, *you*'ve got to watch out for *him*.
(first   (second   (third
person) person)   person)

The term *nominative* refers to forms used in subject position; the term *accusative* refers to forms used in object position (direct object, object of preposition, indirect object).

	Nominative (noun)	Accusative (noun)	1st Possessive (noun determiner)	2nd Possessive (noun)
Singular				
1st person	I	me	my	mine
2nd person	you	you	your	yours
3rd person	he	him	his	his
	she	her	her	hers
	it	it	its	its
Plural				
1st person	we	us	our	ours
2nd person	you	you	your	yours
3rd person	they	them	their	theirs

The following examples illustrate the fact that the "first possessive" functions as a *noun determiner*, while the "second possessive" functions as a *noun*:

Noun determiner	Noun
That's *my* elephant.	That's *mine.*
Her candy is delicious.	*Hers* is delicious.
We bought *their* book.	We bought *theirs.*
I don't like *his* solution.	I don't like *his.*

Note that in the last pair of examples, the form is the same (*his*) for both functions. The same is true of the neuter possessive, *its.*

Noun Determiners

A *noun determiner* has one function: to signal that a noun is to follow. However, a determiner may be separated from its noun by intervening adjectives:

That	wrinkled	old	elephant	is	Ebenezer.
(noun determiner)	(adjectives)		(noun)		

At first glance, noun determiners look very much like adjectives because both must refer to a noun. Unlike adjectives, however, noun determiners cannot be preceded by *very*. We can say: Myrna is very *pretty* (adjective); we can't say: Myrna is very *the* (noun determiner).

There are various kinds of determiners, predeterminers, and postdeterminers. Here we will list just five categories:

1. *Articles*: definite, *the*; indefinite, *a* or *an*. The articles are an infallible signal that a noun will follow.

2. *Demonstratives*: this, these; that, those. As discussed above under "Pronouns," these words can function either as nouns or as noun determiners: Ebenezer likes *these* (noun); Ebenezer likes *these* peanuts (noun determiner).

3. *Possessives*: my, our, your, his, her, its, and *their*. For examples, see again the preceding section on "Pronouns." Note that *his* and *its* can function either as nouns or as noun determiners.

4. *Cardinal numbers*: one, two, three, and so forth. The cardinal numbers can also function as nouns. For example, compare: Helen bought *two* (noun). Helen bought *two* jackets (noun determiner).[23]

5. *Miscellaneous*:

all	every	much
another	either	no
any	few	neither
both	many	other
each	more	several
	most	some

Articles, demonstratives, and possessives are mutually exclusive. Thus, they are sometimes called *regular noun determiners*.

Verbs and Their Auxiliaries

Verbs

A *verb* is traditionally defined as a word that expresses action or a state of being or becoming. Structurally, a verb may be defined as any word which takes a verb ending or a distinctive verb form. There are four kinds of inflectional endings by which many verbs can be identified: *third singular present tense, past tense, present participle,* and *past participle.* These are illustrated below:

Third singular present tense, -s or -es:	He *plays* the piano. He *wishes* he could play the piano.
Past tense, -ed:	He *played* well.
Present participle, -ing:	He is *playing* the piano.
Past participle, -ed:	He has *played* the piano for years.

The third singular ending is used when the verb is present tense and the subject is a singular noun or nominal other than *I* or *you*: He *plays* the piano, That bully *plays* the piano. Otherwise, the present tense verb has no ending: I *play* the piano, Those bullies *play* the piano. Note that in all these cases, the action is habitual rather than presently occurring; to indicate a present action, we would say, for example, He is *playing* the piano. For regular verbs, the past participle form is the same as the past tense form, both ending in -ed. For irregular verbs, there are usually different past tense and past participle forms: *went* versus *gone, sang* versus *sung, ate* versus *eaten,* and so forth. In any case, the past participle may be defined as the form used after a *have* auxiliary (a form of the verb "to have"): He has *played* the piano for years, They have *gone* already, Marvin had *sung* that song many times before.

There are only a few derivational endings that can be used to identify verbs. The following words illustrate almost all of the possibilities: *complicate, amplify, finish, idolize*. Note that *-ate* can also be an adjective ending (That's a *duplicate* key) or a noun ending (Get me a *duplicate*). The *-ish* ending can signal an adjective (as in *childish* and *foolish*).

A verb functions as the head word of a predicate: Ebenezer *snores*, Ebenezer *became* king, Ebenezer *eats* peanuts. As the first example suggests, a verb is the one absolutely essential part of a predicate.

A *verb* may be defined as any word which takes a verb ending or a distinctive verb form. This definition includes three kinds of auxiliary verbs, discussed below. Thus we may have a *verbal phrase*, consisting of a *main verb* preceded by one or more *auxiliary verbs*; He *should leave*, He *should have left*, He *should be leaving*, and so forth.

Verb Auxiliaries

There are three major kinds of *auxiliary verbs* that may precede a main verb. These three kinds are as follows:

Modal		Form of *Have*	Form of *Be*
		(the verb "to have")	(the verb "to be")
can	could	have	be
shall	should	has	am
will	would	had	is
may	might	having	are
must			was
			were
			been
			being

Two and even three auxiliaries may precede a main verb, but they must always occur in this order: modal, form of *have*, form of *be*. Here are some of the many possibilities: She *should have been* driving the jeep, She *should be* driving the jeep, She *had been* driving the jeep, She *was* driving the jeep, She *should have* driven the jeep, She *had* driven the jeep, She *should* drive the jeep. Note that if a form of *have* occurs in the auxiliary, the next word will always be a past participle (by definition). If a form of *be* occurs in the auxiliary, the next word will be a present participle (unless the sentence is passive). The first auxiliary is either in the present or the past tense form.[24] If there is no auxiliary, then the main verb is in either the present or the past tense form.

Adjectives

An *adjective* is traditionally defined as a word that modifies a noun. Structurally, an adjective may be defined as any word that takes an adjective ending or that may be preceded by *more* and *most*. (We will see that some words which may be preceded by *more* and *most* can function either as adjectives or as adverbs.)

Many adjectives can add the inflectional endings -*er* and -*est*, while others express the same meanings by taking *more* and *most*:

Myrna is *pretty*.	Myrna is *beautiful*.
Myrna is *prettier* than Myrtle.	Myrna is *more beautiful* than Myrtle.
Myrna is the *prettiest* turtle I know.	Myrna is the *most beautiful* turtle I know.

Forms like *prettier* and *more beautiful* are called the *comparative degree*: they are used when comparing two entities (e.g. Myrna and Myrtle). Forms like *prettiest* and *most beautiful* are called the *superlative degree*: they are used when comparing three or more entities (Myrna and all other turtles).

There are also several derivational endings by which some adjectives may be identified. The following words illustrate some common derivational endings for adjectives: *adorable, fatal, important, molecular, arbitrary, confident, helpful, fantastic, childish, active, friendless, friendly, gracious, crazy*. Note that the -*ly* ending appears much less often on adjectives than on adverbs (*quickly, slowly, carefully*, and so forth). The -*ant* ending can also be found on nouns (*claimant, coolant*).

As indicated, an adjective functions to modify (describe) a noun. Thus the base form of a true adjective will fit into both of the two major adjective positions: (1) before a noun; and (2) in predicate adjective position, preceded by the word *very*:

That *pretty* turtle is Myrtle.
Myrtle is very *pretty*.

As the example indicates, a *predicate adjective* is an adjective that occurs in the predicate part of the sentence but modifies the subject.

In summary, then, we can define an *adjective* as any word that takes an adjective ending or that can be preceded by *more* and *most*. Any word or construction that functions like an adjective can be called an *adjectival*. An adjectival can consist of a word, a phrase, a near-clause, or a clause. The major kinds of adjectivals may be illustrated as follows:

Word

Adjective:

Pretty turtles are my weakness.

Myrna and Myrtle are *pretty.*

I want something *pretty.*

Noun:[25]

This is *Jane's* coat.

Jack shut the *barn* door.

I like that *grass* skirt.

Adverb:

The man *inside* stole the money.

Verb (participle):

The woman *coughing* should see a doctor.

We'll never recover the money *stolen.*

Phrase

Adjective phrase:

I want something *unusually pretty.*

Noun phrase:[26]

Here is Ms. Anderson, *our president.*

Our president, *Ms. Anderson,* has just arrived.

Adverb phrase:

Those hills *up ahead* aren't mountains.

Prepositional phrase:

That bird *in the tree* is a bluejay.

Verb phrase (participial):

That woman *coughing so hard* should see a doctor.

We'll never recover the money *stolen in yesterday's robbery.*

Near-clause

Absolute:[27]

Albert glared at her angrily, *his eyes black with hate.*

Clause

Adjective clause:

Ebenezer likes the peanuts *that John brings him.*

Turtles *that are pretty* are my weakness.

This is the coat *that Jane has.*

I like that skirt *which is made of grass.*

The man *that is inside* stole the money.

We'll never recover the money *that was stolen.*

I want something *which is unusually pretty.*

Here is Ms. Anderson, *who is our president.*

> Those hills *which are up ahead* aren't mountains.
>
> That bird *which is in the tree* is a bluejay.
>
> That woman *who is coughing so hard* should see a doctor.
>
> Albert, *whose eyes were black with hate*, stared at her angrily.

One further point about adjectival clauses is that there are two basic types, traditionally termed *restrictive* and *nonrestrictive*. Basically, a *restrictive* clause is one that the speaker or writer considers essential for identifying the noun described:

> Matt hates grammar *which isn't clear*.

This says that Matt hates *unclear* grammar; perhaps Matt is a teacher who hates to read papers with poorly constructed sentences. The adjectival clause is restrictive, or essential; it is needed to clarify what kind of grammar Matt hates. In contrast, we have the nonrestrictive clause below:

> Matt hates grammar, *which isn't clear*.

This says that Matt hates grammar—period. Grammar is unclear. The adjectival clause is not needed to clarify what kind of grammar Matt hates: he hates *all* grammar. Hence the clause is called nonrestrictive, or nonessential. A nonrestrictive clause is set off by commas in writing or by distinctive pauses in speech.

Adverbs

An *adverb* is traditionally defined as a word that modifies a verb, an adjective, or another adverb. Structurally, an adverb may be defined as any word that takes an adverb ending or that can function adverbially and be modified by *more* and *most*. Since this structural definition does not encompass many of the words traditionally considered to be adverbs, we will eventually "define" the class of adverbs through examples.

Like adjectives, a few adverbs can add the inflectional endings *-er* and *-est*, while others express the same comparative and superlative meanings by taking *more* and *most*:

Walk *slow*.	Speak *softly*.
Walk *slower*.	Speak *more softly*.
Walk the *slowest* you can.	Speak the *most softly* you can.[28]

Adverbs which have comparative and superlative forms illustrate one of the major types of adverb, the *manner adverb*. These generally answer the question *How?*

There are only four derivational suffixes by which some adverbs may be identified. These may be illustrated as follows: *quickly, slowly; backward(s), forward(s); lengthways, sideways;* and *lengthwise, sidewise*. The *-ly* ending is by far the most common (there is an adjectival *-ly* also, as in *friendly* and *manly*). Adverbs that take derivational endings are also manner adverbs.

As already indicated, an adverb is traditionally said to modify a verb, an adjective, or another adverb:

Walk *slow(ly)*
↑   ↑
(verb) (adverb)

I want something *unusually* pretty.
                          ↑   ↖
                    (adverb)   (adjective)

Walk *really* slow.
↑   ↑
(adverb) (adverb)

Even more often, however, adverbs function to modify entire clauses:

> He *slowly* pulled his sweater on.
>
> *Slowly,* he pulled his sweater on.
>
> He pulled his sweater on *slowly.*

The mobility of *slowly* suggests that it modifies not just the verb, but the whole action of pulling on the sweater.[29]

The category "adverb" is often considered to include not only words that take adverb endings (all of which are manner adverbs) but other words used to modify a verb, adjective, adverb, or clause. An adverb most commonly tells *when, where,* or *how* an action is done. Here are some typical adverbs.

Time adverbs	Place adverbs	Manner adverbs
(*When*)	(*Where*)	(*How*)
today	here	quickly
tomorrow	there	slowly
yesterday	everywhere	backwards
		lengthways
		sidewise

The term *adverb*, then, may be used to describe any word that takes an adverb ending, plus any word which describes when, where, or how an action is done.[30] An *adverbial* is any word or construction that functions like an adverb: to modify an adjective, adverb, verb, or entire clause.

The main function of adverbs is to modify verbs and entire clauses. The chart below indicates both the meanings that adverbials typically express, and the kinds of constructions that typically serve as adverbials. For a fuller discussion of adverb clauses and the subordinators that introduce them, see "Adverbialization" in the section on English Grammar as Process.

Time (answers the question *When?*)

Adverb:	We cleaned the garage *yesterday.*
Noun phrase:	He leaves *this Friday.*
Prepositional phrase:	He leaves *on Friday.*
Adverb clause:	Wash your hands *before we eat dinner.*
	He soaked his toupee *while he was shaving.*[31]

Place (answers the question *Where?*)

Adverb:	We ate *there.*
Prepositional phrase:	He is *at home.*
Adverb clause:	I'd like to go *where Robin went.*
	I'll go *wherever you go.*

Manner (answers the question *How?* More specifically, manner adverbs may answer such questions as *In what manner? How much? By what means? By whom?*)

Adverb:	Walk *slow(ly).* He admired her *greatly.*
Adverb phrase:	Walk *really slow.* He liked her *too much.*
Prepositional phrase:	We lifted it *with care.*
	That was painted *by a new method.*
	That was painted *by Jones.*
Adverb clause:	He cried *as if his heart would break.*
	She sang *like she had never sung before.*

Reason (answers the question *Why?*)

Adverb near-clause (absolute)[32]	*Dinner being almost over,* he didn't stay.
	The door being locked, we can't get in.

Adverb clause:	He didn't stay, *because dinner was almost over.*
	Since the door is locked, we can't get in.

Contrast

Adverb clause:	We don't know them, *(al)though they've lived here three years.*
	Don't laugh, *even though he does look funny.*

Condition

Adverb clause:	We won't leave *if it's snowing.*
	He won't leave *unless you fire him.*

Clauses and Their Related Function Words

Before discussing clauses, we should try to define the term "sentence." As previously noted, there have been many attempts to define this term. Without trying to review these, we will simply define "sentence" as follows:

> *Grammatically,* a *sentence* consists of an independent clause plus whatever dependent clauses may be attached to it or embedded within it.[33]

> *Rhetorically,* a *sentence* may be defined as whatever occurs between the initial capital letter and the final period, or between the onset of speech and the utterance-final pause. Hence a rhetorical sentence may be as short as a single word, or as long as several hundred words.

Having thus laid the groundwork, we can clarify the former definition by discussing independent and dependent clauses.

Earlier, we explained that a clause consists of a noun or other nominal (*someone* or *something*) about which something is predicated. These two parts of the clause have traditional names: the *subject* and the *predicate*, respectively. An *independent* or *main clause*, then, is a subject-plus-predicate construction that can stand alone as a sentence. Below are some examples:

> Ebenezer snores.
> Ebenezer is king.
> Ebenezer eats peanuts.
> John will bring him peanuts.

There are two kinds of words used to join independent clauses: *conjunctive adverbs*, and *coordinating conjunctions*. The words that most commonly function as conjunctive adverbs are as follows: *accordingly, also, anyhow, anyway, besides, consequently, furthermore, hence, however, indeed, likewise, moreover, namely, nevertheless, otherwise, still, then,* and *therefore.*[34] The coordinating conjunctions are as follows: *and, but, for, nor, or, so.*[35] Below are some examples of how these two kinds of words are used to join independent clauses:

> George couldn't see anything; *nevertheless,* he plunged ahead recklessly.
> George couldn't see anything! He plunged ahead recklessly, *nevertheless.*
> George couldn't see anything, *but* he plunged ahead recklessly.
> George couldn't see anything. But he plunged ahead recklessly.

As these examples indicate, the coordinating conjunctions and conjunctive adverbs may be punctuated and positioned differently. Another difference is that the coordinating conjunctions can join not just independent clauses, but also words (Those are my books *and* magazines), phrases (We ran in one door *but* out the other), and dependent clauses (We won't leave if it's snowing *or* if it's raining).

Having defined an independent clause as a subject-plus-predicate construction that can stand alone as a sentence, we logically define a *dependent* or *subordinate* clause as a subject-plus-predicate construction that *cannot* stand alone as a sentence. There are three types of dependent clauses: a *noun clause*, an *adjective clause*, and an *adverb clause*.

A *noun clause* functions like a noun: as subject of a clause, direct object of a verb, predicate nominative, object of a preposition, or (occasionally) indirect object. It is introduced by a *complementizer* (*that, if, whether*) or by a *WH-word* (mainly *who, what, which, when, where, why, how*). Note that a complementizer is simply placed in front of a subject-plus-predicate construction, whereas a WH-word is an integral part of that construction:

> Ebenezer thinks *that John will bring him peanuts.*
> Ebenezer wonders *if John will bring him peanuts.*
> Ebenezer wonders *who will bring him peanuts.*
> Ebenezer wonders *what John will bring him.*

An *adjective clause* functions like an adjective: to modify a noun. An adjective clause is introduced by a *relative pronoun* (mainly *that, who* for humans and pets, *which* for other animates and for inanimates, and *whose* for possessives). Note that the relative pronoun is an integral part of an adjectival clause:

Turtles *that are pretty* are my weakness.
The man *that is inside* stole the money.
The woman *who is coughing* should see a doctor.
I want something *which is unusually pretty.*
Albert, *whose eyes were black with hate,* glared at her angrily.

An *adverb clause* functions like an adverb. Usually an adverb clause
modifies an independent clause. An adverb clause is introduced by a
subordinating conjunction. Note that a subordinating conjunction is
simply placed in front of a subject-plus-predicate unit to make an
adverb clause:

Wash your hands *before we eat dinner.*
He soaked his toupee *while he was shaving.*
I'd like to go *where Robin went.*
He cried *as if his heart would break.*
He didn't stay, *because dinner was almost over.*
We don't know them, *(al)though they've lived here three years.*
We won't leave *if it's snowing.*

Among the most common subordinating conjunctions are the following:
*after, although, as, as if, because, before, even though, if, like, since, so
(that), though, till, unless, until, when, where, wherever, whether (or
not),* and *while.*

Basic Sentence Patterns

There are three basic sentence patterns underlying all others:

1. *Subject + Intransitive verb (+ Adverb)*

   Ebenezer snores.
   Ebenezer snores loudly.

   The parentheses indicate that the adverb is an optional element
   in this basic sentence pattern. An *intransitive verb* is simply a
   verb which is followed by nothing or by an adverb, as above.

2. *Subject + Transitive verb + Direct object*

   Ebenezer eats peanuts.

   A *transitive verb* is simply a verb which is followed by a direct
   object. One way of expanding this pattern is by adding an
   indirect object between the verb and the direct object:

   John gave Ebenezer peanuts.
   John bought Ebenezer peanuts.

Another way is by adding an *objective complement* after the direct object:

John crowned Ebenezer king.

The word *king* is the objective complement. The objective complement refers to the same real world entity as the direct object.

3. *Subject + Linking verb + Subjective complement*
A *subjective complement* is simply a predicate nominative or predicate adjective referring back to the subject. Hence the following sentences illustrate this basic pattern:

Ebenezer is king. (predicate nominative)
Ebenezer is kingly. (predicate adjective)

8 Grammar as Process

This section presents a brief description of English grammar as process, of how sentences are formed. The discussion draws mainly upon transformational grammar.

As noted in the section on comparing grammars, a primary aim of transformational grammar is to account for native speakers' intuitions about their language. In so doing, transformationalists construct grammars that demonstrate, step by step, how sentences can be constructed. Of course the transformationalists realize, and even insist, that their process grammars are not an accurate reflection of how people actually produce or perceive sentences. Nevertheless, the groundwork laid by these linguists is being drawn upon in efforts to determine some of the interrelationships between thought and language.

Turning to meaning, transformationalists point out that sentences express basic *propositions*. A proposition expresses a state or action and the entities involved in that state or action. Or, to put it another way, a proposition makes a statement about an entity. This is somewhat akin to the way we have defined a clause, yet there is a tremendous difference between the term "clause" (a grammatical term) and the term "proposition" (a term of meaning). Let us look at the following sentences:

> The elephant eats peanuts.
> The wrinkled old elephant eats peanuts.

The first sentence consists of one clause and reflects one proposition; we are making one statement about the elephant, namely that it eats peanuts. The second sentence also consists of just one clause, but here we are making *three* statements about the elephant: that it eats peanuts, that it is wrinkled, and that it is old. Hence the second sentence reflects not just one proposition, but three.

Transformationalists are interested in the processes whereby these propositions, these *deep structure sentences*, may be combined and converted into *surface structure sentences*. It is these processes or *transformations* that have given transformational grammar its name.

The term *embedding* describes the process by which we can convert an underlying sentence into a nominal, adjectival, or adverbial and then

122

insert that construction in or attach it to another underlying sentence. We can use the term *insert* to describe the sentence which is converted into a nominal, adjectival, or adverbial. The term *receiver* describes the sentence that accepts the insert. Both inserts and receivers can be described as *underlying sentences*. An underlying sentence is not necessarily "basic," reflecting just one proposition; it may already contain the result of one or more embedding processes. The result of such a process, the transformationally derived nominal, adjectival, or adverbial, may also be called an *embedding*.

The three basic embedding processes are *nominalization, adjectivalization*, and *adverbialization*. We will review each of these in a very nontechnical way, beginning with *adjectivalization* because this process reveals the essence of a transformational grammar in particular and of human language in general. After discussing these three embedding processes we will briefly turn to *coordination*, the process of joining two underlying sentences of the same structure. Then, finally, we will discuss some of the *simple transformations* that can be performed upon a sentence: the *negative, yes/no question, WH-word question, emphasis, passive, cleft, there*, and *it-inversion* transformations.

Adjectivalization

Adjectivalization, the process of creating an adjectival from an underlying sentence, is at the heart of a transformational grammar. It is this process which reflects, more than any other, the *recursive* nature of our language and of human languages in general: the fact that from a finite number of elements and rules we can create a potentially infinite number of sentences. This is relatively easy to demonstrate:

> John likes the old elephant.
> John likes the old, old elephant.
> John likes the old, old, old elephant.

Theoretically there is no limit to the number of times we can repeat the embedding process, adding again and again the proposition "The elephant is old."

The process of adjectivalization illustrates, too, another important fact about human languages: that there are often two or more ways of saying essentially the same thing. Compare, for example, the following sentences:

> John likes the elephant which is old.
> John likes the old elephant.

Both of these sentences express the same two propositions: that John likes the elephant, and that the elephant is old. Thus the two sentences are *paraphrases* of one another. A transformational grammar accounts for such paraphrase relationships by deriving the different surface sentences from the same underlying deep structures.

The process of adjectivalization transforms a sentence into an adjective clause, also called a *relative clause*, which can often be reduced to a phrase or a word.

Restrictive Relative Clauses

A restrictive relative clause is one that the speaker or writer considers essential for identifying the noun described, as in: Matt hates grammar *which isn't clear*. The restrictive clause is not set off by commas in writing or by distinctive pauses in speech.

Below are sets of *receiver* sentences and *insert* sentences. The S in the receiver sentence stands for "sentence" and indicates where the insert is to go. In each case, the insert sentence will be made into a restrictive relative clause modifying the nominal which precedes the S in the receiver. The basic procedure is as follows: find an instance of essentially the same nominal in the insert sentence, replace this nominal with an appropriate relative pronoun, and move the relative pronoun to the front of the insert sentence. The major relative pronouns are as follows: *that*, *who* (and its object form *whom*), *which*, and *whose*. The relative pronoun *that* can replace any nominal except a possessive. *Who* is used mainly for humans and pets; *which* is used for most other animates and for inanimates; and *whose* is used for possessives. For brevity, just the relatives *that* and *those* will be used in the examples below.[36]

1. Receiver: Ebenezer likes *the peanuts* + S.
    Insert: ~~The peanuts~~ *that* crack open easily.
    Result: Ebenezer likes the peanuts *that crack open easily.*

2. Receiver: Ebenezer likes *the peanuts* + S.
    Insert: John brings him ~~the peanuts~~ *(that)*.
    Result: Ebenezer likes the peanuts *that John brings him.*

3. Receiver: That's *the boy* + S.
    Insert: ~~The boy~~ *that* brings peanuts to Ebenezer.
    Result: That's the boy *that brings peanuts to Ebenezer.*

4. Receiver: That's *the boy* + S *(that)*.
    Insert: The elephant loves ~~the boy~~.
    Result: That's the boy *that the elephant loves.*

5. Receiver: That's *the boy* + S.
   Insert: ~~The boy's~~ *whose* peanuts were stolen.
   Result: That's the boy *whose peanuts were stolen.*

As you may have noticed, the relative pronoun can be deleted when it has replaced an object in the insert sentence.

The following are some special cases involving *where, when,* and *why.* To save space, the insert is included in parentheses inside the receiver.

1. R and I: That's *the place* (He lives at ~~the place~~ *where*).
   Result: That's the place *where he lives.*
2. R and I: That was *the time* (Sue got promoted at ~~the time~~ *when*).
   Result: That was the time *when Sue got promoted.*
3. R and I: That's *the reason* (He left for ~~the reason~~ *why*).
   Result: That's the reason *why he left.*

Reducible Restrictive Clauses

Restrictive relative clauses can generally be reduced when the relative pronoun is immediately followed by a form of *be.* We simply delete the relative pronoun and the *be* form:

1. R and I: *Turtles* (~~Turtles~~ *that* are pretty) are my weakness.
   Results: Turtles *that are pretty* are my weakness.
   Pretty turtles are my weakness.

Note that regular adjectives must ordinarily be moved to a position before the noun they modify. In terms of meaning, the insert sentence here should be something like *Turtles can be pretty.*

2. R and I: *The man* (~~The man~~ *that* is inside) stole the money.
   Results: The man *that is inside* stole the money.
   The man *inside* stole the money.

Note that we subtly change the meaning of adverbs (as in this case) and of participles (below), if we move them from a post-noun position to a pre-noun position.

3. R and I: We'll never recover *the money* (~~The money~~ *that* was stolen).
   Results: We'll never recover the money *that was stolen.*
   We'll never recover the money *stolen.*
4. R and I: I want *something* (~~Something~~ *that* is unusually pretty).
   Results: I want something *that is unusually pretty.*
   I want something *unusually pretty.*

5. R and I: *Those hills* (~~Those hills~~ *that* are up ahead) aren't moun-
   tains.
   Results: Those hills *that are up ahead* aren't mountains.
   Those hills *up ahead* aren't mountains.
6. R and I: *That bird* (~~That bird~~ *that* is in the tree) is a bluejay.
   Results: That bird *that is in the tree* is a bluejay.
   That bird *in the tree* is a bluejay.
7. R and I: *The woman* (~~The woman~~ *that* is coughing so hard)
   should see a doctor.
   Results: The woman *that is coughing so hard* should see a
   doctor.
   The woman *coughing so hard* should see a doctor.

Restrictive relative clauses containing a form of *have* can sometimes
be reduced to form a *possessive* or a *noun adjunct* (the base form of a
noun functioning adjectivally to modify a following noun). Also, noun
adjuncts can sometimes be derived from sentences containing *is made
of*. Below are some examples:

1. R and I: This is *the coat* (Jane has ~~the coat~~ *(that)*).
   Results: This is the coat *that Jane has*.
   This is *Jane's* coat.
2. R and I: Jack shut *the door* (The barn has ~~the door~~ *(that)*).
   Results: Jack shut the door *that the barn has*.
   Jack shut the *barn's* door.
   Jack shut the *barn* door.
3. R and I: I like *that skirt* (~~That skirt~~ *that* is made of grass).
   Results: I like that skirt *that is made of grass*.
   I like that *grass skirt*.

Nonrestrictive Relative Clauses

A nonrestrictive relative clause is one that the speaker or writer considers nonessential for identifying the noun described, as in: Matt hates
grammar, *which isn't clear*. The nonrestrictive clause is set off by
commas in writing or by distinctive pauses in speech. Note that we
cannot use *that* to introduce nonrestrictive clauses, nor can we ever
delete just the relative pronoun from the result:

1. Receiver: We were worried about *the millage* + S.
   Insert: ~~The millage~~ *which* didn't seem likely to pass.
   Result: We were worried about the millage, *which didn't
   seem likely to pass*.

2. Receiver: We're always being bothered by *my Aunt Mabel* + S.

   Insert: ~~My Aunt Mabel~~ *who* belongs to the John Birch Society.

   Result: We're always being bothered by my Aunt Mabel, *who belongs to the John Birch Society.*

3. Receiver: That car is our *Jaguar* + S.

   Insert: I like ~~our Jaguar~~ *which* best.

   Result: That car is our Jaguar, *which I like best.*

4. Receiver: Sally likes *Cincinnati* + S.

   Insert: Uncle Joe lives in ~~Cincinnati~~ *where*.

   Result: Sally likes Cincinnati, *where Uncle Joe lives.*

Reducible Nonrestrictive Clauses

Nonrestrictive relative clauses can generally be reduced when the relative pronoun is immediately followed by a form of *be*; we simply delete the relative pronoun and the *be* form. The process is the same as for reducing restrictive clauses, except that commas are added before and after the reduction of the nonrestrictive clause. Note that in some of the examples below, it is perhaps obligatory to reduce the full nonrestrictive clause.

In many cases a reduced nonrestrictive can be moved to the front of the sentence, the end of the sentence, or both. In the examples below, the reduced nonrestrictive is given in both these positions as well as immediately after the noun it modifies. You may wish to consider which position seems best in each case, and why. Remember that moving a reduced nonrestrictive is not supposed to change the meaning of the sentence:

1. R and I: *Ruth* (~~Ruth~~ *who* was exhausted) dragged herself up the stairs.

   Results: Ruth, *who was exhausted,* dragged herself up the stairs.
   Ruth, *exhausted,* dragged herself up the stairs.
   Exhausted, Ruth dragged herself up the stairs.
   Ruth dragged herself up the stairs, *exhausted.*

2. R and I: Here is Ms. Anderson (~~Ms. Anderson~~ *who* is our president).

   Results: Here is Ms. Anderson, *who is our president.*
   Here is Ms. Anderson, *our president.*

This reduction is an *appositive* (a noun or noun phrase modifying a preceding noun and usually separated from it by a comma). Note that an appositive cannot be moved without changing the meaning.

3. R and I: *Mark* (~~Mark~~ *who* was above) could see better than I could.

   Results: Mark, *who was above*, could see better than I could.
   Mark, *above*, could see better than I could.
   Above, Mark could see better than I could.
   Mark could see better than I could, *above*.

4. R and I: *Mindy* (~~Mindy~~ *who* was whistling) picked up her backpack.

   Results: Mindy, *who was whistling*, picked up her backpack.
   Mindy, *whistling*, picked up her backpack.
   Whistling, Mindy picked up her backpack.
   Mindy picked up her backpack, *whistling*.

5. R and I: *Rondi* (~~Rondi~~ *who* was happy at last) smiled.

   Results: Rondi, *who was happy at last*, smiled.
   Rondi, *happy at last*, smiled.
   Happy at last, Rondi smiled.
   Rondi smiled, *happy at last*.

6. R and I: *Barber's grocery* (~~Barber's grocery~~ *which* is up ahead) should have some.

   Results: Barber's grocery, *which is up ahead*, should have some.
   Barber's grocery, *up ahead*, should have some.
   Up ahead, Barber's grocery should have some.
   Barber's grocery should have some, *up ahead*.

7. R and I: *Alicia* (~~Alicia~~ *who* was in town for the day) finally came to visit me.

   Results: Alicia, *who was in town for the day*, finally came to visit me.
   Alicia, *in town for the day*, finally came to visit me.
   In town for the day, Alicia finally came to visit me.
   Alicia finally came to visit me, *in town for the day*.

8. R and I: *Alicia* (~~Alicia~~ *who* was choking back the tears) spoke calmly.

   Results: Alicia, *who was choking back the tears*, spoke calmly.
   Alicia, *choking back the tears*, spoke calmly.
   Choking back the tears, Alicia spoke calmly.
   Alicia spoke calmly, *choking back the tears*.

9. R and I: *Albert* (~~Albert's~~ *whose* eyes were black with hate) stared at her angrily.

   Results: Albert, *whose eyes were black with hate*, stared at her angrily.

> Albert, *(his) eyes black with hate*, stared at her angrily.
> *(His) eyes black with hate*, Albert stared at her angrily.
> Albert stared at her angrily, *(his) eyes black with hate*.

This reduced construction is called an *absolute*: it is in effect a sentence with its form of *be* missing. Note that the relative pronoun *whose* can be replaced by an appropriate possessive pronoun, in this case *his*. Also, the word *with* may be added in front of the absolute: *with his eyes black with hate*.

Adverbialization

Adverbialization is the process of creating an adverbial from an under-lying sentence. The result is usually an adverb clause, which normally occurs at the end of a sentence or at the beginning (though it may also be possible for the adverb clause to interrupt the main clause, in which case the adverb clause is set off by commas).

Below are sets of *receiver* sentences and *insert* sentences. Again, the S in the receiver sentence stands for "sentence" and indicates where the insert sentence is to go. Since adverb clauses commonly follow main clauses, the S has been put in this location.

The basic procedure is simple: we merely add an appropriate subordinating conjunction before the insert sentence and combine the adverbial clause with the main clause, the receiver sentence. Below, the adverbial clause is given in both sentence-final position and sentence-initial position. You may wish to consider which position seems better in each case, and why.

1. Receiver: Wash your hands + S.
    Insert:ₐ*before* We eat dinner.
    Results: Wash your hands *before we eat dinner.*
    Before we eat dinner, wash your hands.

2. Receiver: He soaked his toupee + S.
    Insert:ₐ*while* He was shaving.
    Results: He soaked his toupee *while he was shaving.*
    While he was shaving, he soaked his toupee.

3. Receiver: I'd like to go + S.
    Insert:ₐ*where* Robin went.
    Results: I'd like to go *where Robin went.*
    Where Robin went, I'd like to go.

4. Receiver: He cried + S.
    Insert:ᴧ *as if* His heart would break.
    Results: He cried *as if his heart would break*.
    As if his heart would break, he cried.

5. Receiver: He didn't stay + S.
    Insert:ᴧ *because* Dinner was almost over.
    Results: He didn't stay, *because dinner was almost over*.
    Because dinner was almost over, he didn't stay.

6. Receiver: We didn't know them + S.
    Insert:ᴧ *although* They've lived here three years.
    Results: We don't know them, *(al)though they've lived here three years*.
    (Al)though they've lived here three years, we don't know them.

7. Receiver: We won't leave + S.
    Insert:ᴧ *if* It is snowing.
    Results: We won't leave *if it's snowing*.
    If it's snowing, we won't leave.

Below is a list of common subordinating conjunctions, for convenient reference:

Time	Reason
before	because
after	since
since	as
until	so (that)
till	
when	Contrast
while	
as	though
	although
Place	even though
where	Condition
wherever	
	if
Manner	unless
	whether (or not)
as if	
like	

Nominalization

Nominalization is the process of creating a nominal from an underlying sentence. The nominal is then inserted into a noun position in a receiver sentence. Nominals created through this process rarely function as indirect objects, but they occur with some frequency in the other four noun positions: subject, direct object, predicate nominative, and object of a preposition. Direct object position is the most common. The process of nominalization produces two kinds of clauses and three kinds of near-clauses:

Clauses	Near-clauses
WH-word clause	Gerundive
that-clause	Infinitival
	WH-word infinitival

As the term suggests, the WH-word infinitival is a combination of the WH-word and the infinitival.

Each of these will be discussed in turn.

WH-word Clause

To create a WH-word nominal, we replace an indefinite noun, adverb, or noun determiner in the insert sentence with an appropriate WH-word (*who, what, which, whose, when, where, why, how*). The WH-word is moved to the front of the insert, and the insert is then ready to be put into the receiver:

1. Receiver: _____ is a mystery.
   (subject)
   Insert: ~~Someone~~ *who* did it.
   Result: *Who did it* is a mystery.

2. Receiver: Ebenezer wonders _____
   (direct object)
   Insert: He did it *for some reason* *(why)*.
   Result: Ebenezer wonders *why he did it*.

3. Receiver: Ebenezer wonders _____
   (direct object)
   Insert: John will bring him peanuts ~~sometime~~ *(when)*.
   Result: Ebenezer wonders *when John will bring him peanuts*.

4. Receiver: The question is _____
   (predicate nominative)
   Insert: ~~Some~~ *which* kid did it.
   Result: The question is *which kid did it*.

5. Receiver: I'm curious about _____
   (object of preposition)
   Insert: He did it *for some reason* *(why)*.
   Result: I'm curious about *why he did it*.

That-*Clause*

Basically, a *that*-clause nominal is created by putting the complementizer *that* in front of an insert sentence and then putting the resulting construction into the specified position of the receiver. (The process is essentially the same for noun clauses introduced by *if* or *whether*.)

1. Receiver: _____ was amazing.
         (subject)

    Insert:ᴧ *that* He was still able to walk.

    Result: *That he was still able to walk* was amazing.

Note that sentences with a noun clause in subject position are usually awkward. We commonly transpose these into structures like this: It was amazing *that he could still walk.*

2. Receiver: _____ is unbelievable.
         (subject)

    Insert:ᴧ *that* He flies so well.

    Result: *That he flies so well* is unbelievable.

3. Receiver: I regret _____
              (direct object)

    Insert:ᴧ *that* I am not able to go.

    Result: I regret *that I am not able to go.*

4. Receiver: Ebenezer thinks _____
              (direct object)

    Insert:ᴧ *that* John will bring him peanuts.

    Result: Ebenezer thinks *that John will bring him peanuts.*

5. Receiver: The truth is _____
              (predicate nominative)

    Insert:ᴧ *that* He's mean.

    Result: The truth is *that he's mean.*

Note that the complementizer *that* is often deletable if the noun clause is not functioning as a subject. Also, note that some of the sentences above can take *the fact* before the complementizer *that*: I regret *the fact* that I am not able to go. (You might want to consider which sentences can take the *fact*, which cannot, and why). A *that*-clause can serve as the object of a preposition if *that* is preceded by *the fact*:

I'm sorry about *the fact that you lost.*
          (object of preposition)

Usually, however, we would reduce such a construction: I'm sorry *that you lost*; I'm sorry *you lost*.

Gerundive Near-clause

A *gerund* is traditionally defined as the *-ing* form of a verb functioning as a noun, as in: *Swimming* is fun; I like *swimming*. Thus any construction based upon the ground is a *gerundive*. By defintion, the gerundive nominal has as its essential element the *-ing* form of a verb functioning as a noun.

To derive a gerundive, the verb of the insert is changed to the *-ing* form, and various other changes may be made (see the examples below). The subject of the insert usually becomes a possessive determiner, though in some cases the base form of the noun or the object form of the pronoun may be used.

1. Receiver: _____ annoyed Santa.
   (subject)

   Insert: They stayed so late.
   Result: *Their staying so late* annoyed Santa.

2. Receiver: Ebenezer likes _____
   (direct object)

   Insert: John brings him peanuts.
   Result: Ebenezer likes *John's bringing him peanuts*.

3. Receiver: The problem is _____
   (predicate nominative)

   Insert: He has done so badly.
   Result: The problem is *his having done so badly*.

Note that a *have* auxiliary may be transformed into a gerund, as above.

4. Receiver: I was amazed by _____
   (object of preposition)

   Insert: Groucho sang Aida beautifully.
   Result: I was amazed by *Groucho's beautiful singing of Aida*.

Note that all of these gerundives may be paraphrased as *that*-clauses introduced by *the fact*:

The fact that they stayed so late annoyed Santa.
Ebenezer likes *the fact that John brings him peanuts*.
The problem is *the fact that he has done so badly*.
I was amazed by *the fact that Groucho sang Aida beautifully*.

Gerundives can usually be paraphrased as factive *that*-clauses. Conversely, factive *that*-clauses can often be paraphrased as gerundives:

> *The fact that he was still able to walk* was amazing.
> *His still being able to walk* was amazing.
> *The fact that he flies so well* is unbelievable.
> *His flying so well* is unbelievable.
> I regret *the fact that I am not able to go.*
> I regret *not being able to go.*

Infinitival Near-clause

An *infinitive* is traditionally defined as *to* plus the base form of a verb, as in: *To swim* would be nice; I like *to swim*. Thus any construction based upon an infinitive and functioning as a noun is an *infinitival*. By definition, the infinitival nominal has as its essential element the word *to* plus the base form of a verb.

The auxiliary *will* has been included in the insert sentences because infinitivals seem to imply a sense of futurity; however, this is not entirely satisfactory because there is no guarantee that the action expressed by the infinitival will actually be carried out. To derive an infinitival, the auxiliary *will* in the insert is changed to the word *to*, and the word *for* is ordinarily placed in front of the subject of the insert. After the insert has been placed within the receiver, it may be possible to delete the word *for* and, in some cases, to delete the original subject of the insert. The following examples illustrate the major possibilities. The parentheses indicate elements that may be deleted:

1. Receiver: _____ would be a good idea.
         (subject)

   Insert: John will bring Ebenezer peanuts.
   Result: *For John to bring Ebenezer peanuts* would be a
        good idea.

2. Receiver: _____ would be a good idea.
         (subject)

   Insert: Someone will bring Ebenezer peanuts.
   Result: *(For someone) to bring Ebenezer peanuts* would be a
        good idea.

3. Receiver: Ebenezer wants _____
                     (direct object)

   Insert: John will bring him peanuts.
   Result: Ebenezer wants *(for) John to bring him peanuts.*

4. Receiver: John wants _____
        (direct object)

   Insert: John will go to the circus.
   Result: John wants *to go to the circus.*

Note that we would ordinarily delete *for John* from the insert, assuming that the receiver and the insert sentence both refer to the same individual.

5. Receiver: The problem is _____
        (predicate nominative)

   Insert: We will determine the answer.
   Result: The problem is *(for us) to determine the answer.*

6. Receiver: There's no alternative except _____
        (object of preposition)

   Insert: You will agree.
   Result: There's no alternative except *(for you) to agree.*

Note that these infinitivals cannot be paraphrased as a *that*-clause. This is often true of infinitivals.

WH-word Infinitival Near-clause

The *WH-word infinitival* is a combination of the WH-word and the infinitival. By definition, the WH-word infinitival has as its essential elements a WH-word plus an infinitive: *where to go, what to do,* and so forth. The auxiliary *should* has been included in the insert sentences because WH-word infinitivals seem to imply a sense of obligation, or at least of futurity; however, this is not entirely satisfactory because there is no guarantee that the action expressed by the infinitival will actually be carried out.

Since we have already discussed the two basic processes involved, they will simply be illustrated here. Note, however, that this time the word *to* replaces the auxiliary *should*; also, the word *for* and the underlying subject are normally deleted. The first example will illustrate the process in detail:

1. Receiver: _____ is the question.
        (subject)

   Insert: We should go somewhere.

   Process: for us to ~~we should~~ go ~~somewhere~~ (where).
           where ~~for us~~ to go

   Result: *Where to go* is the question.

2. Receiver: He wonders _____
                                         (direct object)

    Insert: He should do *something* after lunch.
    Result: He wonders *what to do after lunch.*

3. Receiver: The question is _____
                                         (predicate nominative)

    Insert: Someone should let go *sometime.*
    Result: The question is *when to let go.*

4. Receiver: He is concerned about _____
                                         (object of preposition)

    Insert: He should buy *some* shirt.
    Result: He is concerned about *what shirt to buy.*

Note that these WH-word infinitivals can be paraphrased as WH-word clauses:

> *Where we should go* is the question.
> He wonders *what he should do after lunch.*
> The question is *when someone should let go.*
> He is concerned about *what shirt he should buy.*

Coordination

Coordination is the process of joining two underlying sentences of the same structure by the use of a *coordinating conjunction: and, but, for, nor, or, so.* Again we will use the terms *receiver* and *insert* in the examples below. If the receiver and insert sentences are partially the same, the repeated part may be deleted from the insert. The parentheses below indicate elements that may be deleted.

1. Receiver: George couldn't see anything.
                    but
    Insert: ∧ George plunged ahead recklessly.
    Result: George couldn't see anything, *but (George) plunged ahead recklessly.*

We would ordinarily omit the second occurrence of *George,* or change the name to *he:* George couldn't see anything, *but he plunged ahead recklessly.*

2. Receiver: Those are my books + S.
                    and
    Insert: ∧ Those are my magazines.
    Result: Those are my books *and (those are my) magazines.*

3. Receiver: We ran in one door + S.
    Insert:∧ We ran out the other door. *(but)*
    Result: We ran in one door *but (we ran) out the other (door)*.

4. Receiver: We won't leave if it's snowing.
    Insert:∧ We won't leave if it's raining. *(or)*
    Result: We won't leave if it's snowing *or (if it's) raining*.

Note that in this case it is obligatory to delete the main subject and verb from the insert, to produce either: We won't leave if it's snowing or if it's raining, or, We won't leave if it's snowing or raining. Otherwise, we would have to restructure the insert sentence and join the two sentences with *nor*: We won't leave if it's snowing, nor will we leave if it's raining.

As we saw in the section on English Grammar as Product, independent clauses can be joined not only by coordinating conjunctions, but also by conjunctive adverbs like *furthermore, however, nevertheless,* and *therefore*.

Simple Transformations

There are several *simple transformations* that can be performed upon a sentence. They are called "simple" because they do not involve the combining of two sentences, but rather are performed upon only one underlying sentence (upon an insert, receiver, or result sentence). We will discuss eight of these simple transformations: the *negative, yes/no question, WH-word question, emphasis, passive, cleft, there,* and *it-inversion* transformations. As described here, the first four of these simple transformations change the meaning of the underlying sentence. This would not generally be true in a more complex transformational grammar, one that deals with underlying elements rather than already-formed sentences. The last four of these simple transformations are stylistic, changing the focus of a sentence rather than its basic meaning.

Of course there are other simple transformations that could be discussed. For example, we could explain the imperative transformation, which derives imperatives like *Close the door* from an underlying sentence with *you* as subject; or we could discuss the transformations that move adverbials and reductions of nonrestrictive adjectival clauses from one location to another in the sentence. But since such transformations are almost self-explanatory, the following discussion will be limited to just those eight transformations listed above.

The Negative Transformation

There are various ways of making a word or a sentence negative, but the basic process of sentence negation is quite straightforward. We merely add the negative marker *not* (or its contraction, *n't*) after the first auxiliary verb. If there is no auxiliary verb, we add an appropriate form of *do* (the verb "to do") and place the negative marker after it. The double arrow indicates a transformation.

> She should have been driving⇒She should *not* have been driv-
> the jeep.   ing the jeep.
> She had been driving the jeep.⇒She had *not* been driving the
>   jeep.
> She was driving the jeep.   ⇒She was *not* driving the jeep.
> She drives the jeep.   ⇒She *does not* drive the jeep.
> We drive the jeep.   ⇒We *do not* drive the jeep.
> They drove the jeep.   ⇒They *did not* drive the jeep.

Note that when we "add an appropriate form of *do*," what we are really doing is moving the tense marker from the main verb to a *do* auxiliary.

The Yes/No Question Transformation

Again there are various ways of asking questions or of questioning elements within a sentence, but the basic process of creating a question that asks for a "Yes" or "No" answer is quite straightforward. We merely move the first auxiliary verb to the front of the sentence. If there is no auxiliary verb, we add an appropriate form of *do* at the beginning of the sentence:

> She should have been driving⇒*Should* she have been driving
> the jeep.   the jeep?
> She has been driving the jeep. ⇒*Has* she been driving the jeep?
> She is driving the jeep.   ⇒*Is* she driving the jeep?
> She drives the jeep.   ⇒*Does* she drive the jeep?
> They drive the jeep.   ⇒*Do* they drive the jeep?
> He drove the jeep.   ⇒*Did* he drive the jeep?

The WH-word Question Transformation

The WH-word question is a question that asks for information, as opposed to a mere "Yes" or "No" answer. The WH-word question begins with a WH-word, usually *who, what, which, where, why,* or *how.* There are two basic steps involved. First, we replace an indefinite noun, noun determiner, or adverb with an appropriate WH-word, and move this WH-word to the front of the sentence. Second, we move the first auxiliary verb to a position immediately after the WH-word; if there is no auxiliary verb, we add an appropriate form of *do*:

~~Someone~~ *who* should have been driv-⇒ *Who* should have been driving
ing the jeep.   the jeep?

She had been driving ~~something~~ *what*.⇒ *What* had she been driving?

She was driving ~~some~~ *which* jeep.   ⇒ *Which* jeep was she driving?

She has driven the jeep ~~some~~ *when*-⇒ *When* has she driven the jeep?
~~time~~.

She drives the jeep ~~somewhere~~ *where*.⇒ *Where* does she drive the jeep?

They drive the jeep ~~for some~~ *why*⇒ *Why* do they drive the jeep?
~~reason~~.

He drove the jeep ~~somehow~~ *how*.   ⇒ *How* did he drive the jeep?

Note that when a noun determiner is moved to the front of the sentence, the noun it modifies must also be moved: *Which* jeep was she driving?

The Emphasis Transformation

Again, there are various ways of emphasizing sentences or parts of sentences. The basic process of sentence emphasis, however, is quite straightforward. We merely emphasize the first auxiliary verb. If there is no auxiliary verb, we add an appropriate form of *do* and emphasize it. In the examples below, the italics indicate the word emphasized:

She should have been driving⇒She *should* have been driving
the jeep.   the jeep.

She has been driving the jeep.⇒She *has* been driving the jeep.

She is driving the jeep.   ⇒She *is* driving the jeep.

She drives the jeep.   ⇒She *does* drive the jeep.

They drive the jeep.   ⇒They *do* drive the jeep.

He drove the jeep.   ⇒He *did* drive the jeep.

The Passive Transformation

The passive transformation changes the style or focus of a sentence more than its basic meaning. In order to perform a passive transformation we must first have a direct object, as in: She drives the jeep. There are three basic steps to the process: (1) the direct object is moved to the front of the sentence, where it becomes the subject; (2) the original subject is moved to the end of the sentence, and *by* is placed before it; (3) an appropriate form of *be* is added before the main verb, and the main verb is put in the past participle form. The total process may be illustrated as follows:

She should have driven the jeep.	⇒ The jeep should have been driven by her.
She had driven the jeep.	⇒ The jeep had been driven by her.
She was driving the jeep.	⇒ The jeep was being driven by her.
She drives the jeep.	⇒ The jeep is driven by her.
She drove the jeep.	⇒ The jeep was driven by her.

We often delete the agent phrase (*by her*, in this case) from the resulting passive.

The Cleft Transformations

Like the passive transformation, the cleft transformations change the style or focus of a sentence rather than its basic meaning. The *what*-cleft transformation can focus attention on any nonhuman noun. The basic process involves three steps: (1) place *what* at the front of the sentence; (2) add *is* or *was* (whichever is appropriate) at the end of the sentence; and (3) move to the end of the sentence the noun phrase to be emphasized. The total process may be illustrated as follows:

The monkey drives the jeep.	⇒ What the monkey drives is the jeep.
The monkey drives the jeep.	⇒ What drives the jeep is the monkey.
The monkey drove the jeep.	⇒ What the monkey drove was the jeep.
The monkey drove the jeep.	⇒ What drove the jeep was the monkey.

The second and fourth result sentences sound rather strange, because a monkey seems more like a "who" than a "what." Oddly enough, we don't have a *who*-cleft comparable to the *what*-cleft; that is, we would not normally say something like: Who drove the jeep was Marvin. However, the *what*-cleft does have its versatility: it can focus attention not only on any nonhuman noun phrase, but also on an entire predicate. This time the basic process involves five steps: (1) place *what* at the front of the sentence; (2) add *do, does,* or *did* (whichever is appropriate) after the subject; (3) add *is* or *was* (whichever is appropriate) after the *do, does,* or *did*; (4) remove the tense marker from the main verb; and (5) move the entire predicate to the end of the sentence. The total process may be illustrated as follows:

The monkeys drive the jeep.	⇒ What the monkeys do is drive the jeep.
The monkey drives the jeep.	⇒ What the monkey does is drive the jeep.
The monkey drove the jeep.	⇒ What the monkey did was drive the jeep.

Another kind of cleft transformation is the *it*-cleft. The process involves first creating a *what*-cleft, then transforming it as follows: (1) add *it* to the left of the *is* or *was* inserted by the *what*-cleft transformation; (2) move everything preceding this *it* to the end of the sentences; and (3) put *that* in place of the *what* added by the *what*-cleft transformation. The total process is easier to illustrate than to explain:

What the monkey drives is the jeep.	⇒ It is the jeep that the monkey drives.
What drives the jeep is the monkey.	⇒ It is the monkey that drives the jeep.
What the monkey drove was the jeep.	⇒ It was the jeep that the monkey drove.
What drove the jeep was the monkey.	⇒ It was the monkey that drove the jeep.

The *it*-cleft transformation may also be applied to *what*-clefts that focus on the predicate rather than on a noun, but the results tend to be somewhat awkward.

The There *Transformation*

The *there* transformation is another that changes style and focus. In most cases, a sentence which has undergone the *there* transformation seems more natural than its untransformed counterpart. This is because the *there* transformation puts all of the important information in the predicate part of the sentence. Generally a sentence will undergo the *there* transformation only if it contains a form of *be* functioning as the main verb or as an auxiliary. There are two basic steps involved: (1) move the *be* form and any preceding auxiliary verbs to the front of the sentence; (2) add the word *there* at the very front of the sentence. The total process may be illustrated as follows:

A mouse is in the closet.	⇒ There is a mouse in the closet.
Some bugs were in the oatmeal.	⇒ There were some bugs in the oatmeal.
A woman is piloting the plane.	⇒ There is a woman piloting the plane.
No one has been in that room.	⇒ There has been no one in that room.

The *there* transformation involves several peculiarities. For example: it appears that the subject of the sentence must have an indefinite determiner, as in the sentences above. Another peculiarity is that the *there* transformation seems obligatory with certain kinds of constructions. We would say *There really are ghosts* rather than *Ghosts really are*; we would say *There is no life after death* rather than *No life after death is*; and we would say *There appeared to be a problem* rather than *A problem appeared to be.* (See Malmstrom and Weaver 1973 for more details concerning the *there* transformation.)

The It-inversion Transformation

The *it*-inversion transformation is also known as the extraposition transformation. It transposes subject nominalizations into the predicate part of the sentence. When a nominalization occurs as the subject of a sentence, the sentence can usually undergo *it*-inversion. The nominalization is moved to the end of the sentence, and *it* is inserted in subject position. The original subject nominalization is italicized in the following examples:

> *Who did it* is a mystery.   ⇒It is a mystery who did it.
>
> *That he was still able to walk* ⇒It was amazing that he was still
> was amazing.   able to walk.
>
> *For John to bring Ebenezer pea-* ⇒It would be a good idea for John
> *nuts* would be a good idea.   to bring Ebenezer peanuts.

The *it*-inversion transformation can usually be performed whenever the subject nominalization is a WH-word clause, a *that*-clause, or an infinitival, as in the examples above. However, gerundives are another matter. Short, uncomplicated gerundives seem to undergo extraposition much more readily than longer, more complicated gerundives. For example, we might well transform *Feeding bears is dangerous* into *It is dangerous feeding bears.* On the other hand, we are not likely to transform *Their staying so late annoyed Santa* into *It annoyed Santa their staying so late.*

9 Grammar as Guidebook

This section suggests how an understanding of grammar can be *useful* in helping writers learn certain conventions of mechanics. Because the following discussion is merely illustrative rather than exhaustive, it deals with only one topic, punctuation, and specifically the punctuation of clauses and their reductions.

This discussion uses some of the terms and examples of the sections on English Grammar as Product and English Grammar as Process, but the organization and tone here are entirely different. The assumed audience is no longer the dispassionate scholar, but the writer (or teacher) seeking advice on how to use the language effectively. Thus the following discussion illustrates the aim of traditional school grammars: to serve as a guidebook to the conventions of educated usage and mechanics.

The Clause, Defined

The purpose of punctuation is psycholinguistic: to signal relationships between thought and language, to divide written language into meaningful chunks for the reader. These chunks are known as the *paragraph*, the *sentence*, the *clause*, the *phrase*, and finally the *word*. Here we will concentrate on the clause, with some attention to larger and smaller units as necessary.

In its most basic form, a *clause* consists of a *noun*-part followed by a *verb*-part. Some nouns are proper names, like *Bob, Joe,* or *Mr. Evans*; others are pronouns, like *I, you, they, someone, nothing.* Most other kinds of nouns can occur after *the: the boy, the street, the dog, the idea.* Usually the most basic form of a verb can occur after *can: can sleep, can stay, can dance, can work.* Putting such noun-parts and verb-parts together, we can create simple clauses like the following:

the boy can sleep
the street can stay
the dog can dance
the idea can work

Of course the noun-part and the verb-part may be much more complicated, but these are the two basic parts of a clause. The noun-part is known as the *subject*. The verb-part is known as the *predicate*.

No matter how complicated, the subject part usually has a single "head" noun, also known as the *simple subject*. The predicate part will have a single "head" verb, also known as the *main verb* or as the *simple predicate*. In the clauses below, the simple subject and the simple predicate (main verb) are italicized:

Subject Part	Predicate Part
the *boy*	can *sleep*
the *street*	can *stay*
the *dog*	can *dance*
the *idea*	can *work*

There are two major kinds of clauses. The first is the *independent clause*, also known as the *main clause*. The independent clause is a subject-plus-predicate construction which can stand alone as a sentence. The clauses above are independent clauses. Below are some more examples:

The elephant sneezes.
The elephant became king.
The elephant eats peanuts.
The baby will bring him peanuts.

The second major kind of clause is the *dependent clause*, also known as the *subordinate clause*. A dependent clause is only a part of a sentence. It functions like an *adjective*, to describe a noun; or it functions like an *adverb* usually does, to describe an action; or it functions like a *noun*. These three kinds of clauses can be briefly illustrated as follows:

Adjective: We brought presents to the elephant *who became king*.
Adverb: *When the elephant sneezes*, everybody runs.
Noun: Everybody knows *that the elephant eats peanuts*.

In the first sentence, *who became king* is an adjective clause describing the noun *elephant*. In the second sentence, *when the elephant sneezes* is an adverb clause telling when everybody runs. In the third sentence, *that the elephant eats peanuts* is a noun clause specifying what everybody knows. We will return later to the adverb and the adjective clause and how to punctuate them. Noun clauses seldom cause problems with punctuation, so they will receive no further attention.

Joining T-units

The next topic is how to join independent clauses and whatever is associated with them. First, however, the term *sentence* should be defined:

> In terms of punctuation, a *sentence* consists of whatever occurs between an initial capital letter and a final period. According to this definition, a sentence may be as short as a single word, or as long as several hundred words.
>
> In grammatical terms, a *sentence* consists of an independent clause plus any dependent clauses that may be attached to it or embedded within it. Thus defined, a sentence is sometimes called a "minimum terminable unit," or *T-unit* for short.

In other words, a grammatical sentence, a T-unit, may consist of just an independent clause, or it may have in addition one or more dependent clauses or their reductions.

When teachers note that what has been punctuated as a sentence is not a sentence, they usually mean that the construction is not a properly formed T-unit, or else it is two or more T-units improperly joined.

So how do we join, or separate, T-units into punctuated sentences? Basically there are five ways:

1. *With a period.* Think of a period as a full stop, dividing T-units rather than joining them.

    I came. I saw. I conquered.

2. *With a semicolon.* Think of a semicolon as a semi-stop, joining T-units rather loosely.

    I came; I saw; I conquered.

    The semicolon implies a closer connection between the T-units than the period does. The semicolon is most comfortable in formal writing. Even there, it is used sparingly.

3. *With a comma.* Think of a comma as a significant pause, joining T-units very tightly.

    I came, I saw, I conquered.

    As this example demonstrates, it can be quite effective to join T-units with commas, particularly if there are three short T-units in a series. Usually, however, it is considered improper to join T-units with only a comma. This is called a *comma splice*, also known as a *run-on* sentence. An example might be:

    The elephant sneezes, everybody runs.

4. *With a comma plus a coordinating conjunction.* To repair the above comma splice, we might simply add the word *and*:

The elephant sneezes, *and* everybody runs.

The coordinating conjunctions which work in this way are *and*, *but*, *for*, *nor*, *or*, and *so*. The most common are *and* and *but*, with *or* running a poor third:

The elephant sneezes, *and* everybody runs.

The elephant sneezes, *but* nobody runs.

The elephant had better sneeze, *or* nobody will come visit him anymore.

The comma can often be omitted if the two T-units are short:

The elephant sneezes *and* everybody runs.

The elephant sneezes *but* nobody runs.

Incidentally, you can start sentences with *and* or *but*:

The elephant sneezed. *And* then it happened.

The elephant sneezed. *But* nothing happened.

It's best, however, to use the initial *and* or *but* sparingly, for special effect.

5. *With a semicolon plus a conjunctive adverb* (or a period plus a conjunctive adverb). The conjunctive adverbs are strange creatures, expressing a variety of meanings. The most common are as follows:

accordingly	furthermore	namely
also	hence	nevertheless
anyhow	however	otherwise
anyway	indeed	still
besides	likewise	then
consequently	moreover	therefore

These may combine with a semicolon to join two T-units, as the following examples illustrate:

That can't be the right explanation; *indeed*, it's hardly an explanation at all.

We haven't solved the problem yet; *however*, the answer must be here somewhere.

We'd better keep trying these combinations; *otherwise*, we may miss something vital.

Note that instead of a semicolon, we can often have a period in front of the T-unit containing the conjunctive adverb:

That can't be the right explanation. *Indeed*, it's hardly an explanation at all.

We haven't solved the problem yet. *However*, the answer must be here somewhere.

We'd better keep trying these combinations. *Otherwise* we may miss something vital.

Note also that some conjunctive adverbs can be moved within their T-unit. Most of these connectors must be set off by commas from the rest of their T-unit, but some can take the commas or do without:

However, the answer must be here somewhere.

The answer, *however*, must be here somewhere.

The answer must be here somewhere, *however*.

Otherwise, we may miss something vital.

We may miss something vital, *otherwise*.

Otherwise we may miss something vital.

We may miss something vital *otherwise*.

In deciding whether or not to use commas to set off a conjunctive adverb, remember that a comma signals a significant pause.

In summary, then, there are five basic ways of joining two T-units.

1. *With a period.*
2. *With a semicolon.*
3. *With a comma* (usually not recommended).
4. *With a comma plus a coordinating conjunction.*
5. *With a semicolon plus a conjunctive adverb* (or with a period plus a conjunctive adverb).

The first way is the most common.

Adding Dependent Clauses or Their Reductions

Earlier we noted that there are three types of dependent clauses, two of which are added to describe or "modify" the entire main clause or some part of it. One of these is the *adverb clause*, which usually describes the action indicated in the main clause. The other is the *adjective clause*, which describes some noun in the main clause. We will discuss each of these in turn, showing how they are punctuated.

Adverb Clauses and Their Reductions

As already noted, the *adverb clause* usually describes the action indicated in the main clause. On the rare occasions when an adverb clause interrupts the main clause, it is set off by commas. If an adverb clause occurs before the main clause, it is followed by a comma. If an adverb clause follows the main clause, it is often preceded by a comma, but not always. In deciding whether or not to put a comma before a final adverb clause, consider whether it is natural for your reader to pause. The examples below illustrate these conventions of punctuation and suggest the various meanings typically conveyed by adverb clauses:

Time (answers the question *when?*)

Before we eat dinner, you'd better wash your hands. (comma required)

You'd better wash your hands *before we eat dinner*. (comma optional)

While he was shaving, he soaked his toupee. (comma required)

He soaked his toupee *while he was shaving*. (comma optional)

He soaked his toupee *while shaving*. (comma is optional in this reduction of the adverb clause)

Place (answers the question *where?*)

I'd like to go *where Robin went*. (comma omitted)

Wherever you go, I'll go. (comma required)

I'll go *wherever you go*. (comma likely to be omitted)

Manner (answers the question *how?*)

He cried *as if his heart would break*. (comma likely to be omitted)

She sang *like she had never sung before*. (comma likely to be omitted)

Reason (answers the question *why?*)

Because dinner was almost over, he didn't stay. (comma required)

Dinner being almost over, he didn't stay. (comma required in this reduction of the adverb clause)

He didn't stay, *because dinner was almost over*. (comma likely)

He didn't stay, *dinner being almost over*. (comma required in this reduction of the adverb clause)

Since the door is locked, we can't get in. (comma required)

The door being locked, we can't get in. (comma required in this reduction of the adverb clause)

We can't get in, *since the door is locked*. (comma required)

We can't get in, *the door being locked*. (comma required in this reduction of the adverb clause)

Contrast

Although they've been here three years, we don't know them. (comma required)

We don't know them, *although they've been here three years*. (comma required)

Even though he does look funny, don't laugh. (comma required)

Don't laugh, *even though he does look funny*. (comma required)

Condition

> *If it's snowing,* we won't leave. (comma required)
> We won't leave *if it's snowing.* (comma optional)
> The truth, *if you want to know,* is that he's lazy. (commas required)
> *Unless you fire him,* he won't leave. (comma required)
> He won't leave *unless you fire him.* (comma optional)

As these examples suggest, the adverb clause occurs most commonly and most comfortably in final position.

You may have noticed that an adverb clause consists of a subject-plus-predicate construction preceded by a word like *before, because,* or *if.* When these words introduce adverb clauses, they are called *subordinating conjunctions,* or *subordinators* for short. Below is a list of common subordinators, for convenient reference:

Time	Reason
before	because
after	since
since	as
until	so (that)
till	
when	**Contrast**
while	though
as	although
	even though
Place	
where	**Condition**
wherever	if
	unless
Manner	whether (or not)
as if	
like	

Some constructions that function like adverbs do not seem to be reductions of a clause, but they are punctuated similarly. The most common is the prepositional phrase functioning adverbially.(A *prepositional phrase* consists of a noun or noun-headed construction preceded by a preposition, a word like *at, by, for, from, in, of, on, to,* and *with.*) If a long prepositional phrase comes before a main clause, it is likely to be followed by a comma. If the prepositional phrase is short, it is usually not followed by a comma. Examples:

> *In a few hundred years from now,* we'll know the answer.
> *In a moment* we'll know the answer.

As these sentences suggest, whether or not you use a comma depends mainly on whether or not it would be natural for the reader to pause after the introductory prepositional phrase. The same is true for adverbially functioning prepositional phrases interrupting the main clause or coming afterwards. To pause or not to pause: that is the question. Again, some examples:

> We should know, *in a moment*, the final answer.
> We should know *in a moment* the final answer.
> We should know the final answer, *in a moment*.
> We should know the final answer *in a moment*.

As these sentences suggest, such prepositional phrases occur most comfortably before or after the main clause rather than in the middle.

Doubltess we should say a word about *sentence fragments*, a teacher's common complaint. When teachers note that a student has used a sentence fragment, they may mean that the student has punctuated an adverb clause as if it were a complete T-unit:

> He finally won the race. *After he had practiced for many years.*
> He knew he could win. *Because he was in top condition.*
> Please come visit us. *If you can.*

In each case, the sentence fragment can be repaired by joining the adverbial clause to the main clause it modifies.

> He finally won the race, *after he had practiced for many years.*
> He knew he could win, *because he was in top condition.*
> Please come visit us, *if you can.*

Another type of adverbial that is commonly punctuated as a sentence is illustrated below:

> He didn't stay. *Dinner being almost over.*
> We can't get in. *The door being locked.*

The problem here is the participle form *being*; it is seldom used as a main verb, and only then with an appropriate helper as in: David *is being* silly. There are three basic ways to repair such a sentence fragment. One is simply to join the adverbial to the main clause it modifies.

> He didn't stay, *dinner being almost over.*
> We can't get in, *the door being locked.*

A second way is to change the word *being* to the appropriate form of *to be* (*am*, *is*, *are*, *was*, or *were*):

> He didn't stay. *Dinner was almost over.*
> We can't get in. *The door is locked.*

A third way is to make the adverbial into a full clause and attach it to the main clause:

> He didn't stay, *because dinner was almost over.*
> We can't get in, *since the door is locked.*

Adjective Clauses and Their Reductions

As noted earlier, an *adjective clause* describes some noun in the main clause. There are two major types of adjective clauses, the restrictive clause and the nonrestrictive clause.

Basically, a *restrictive clause* is one that the speaker or writer considers essential for identifying the noun described:

> Matt hates grammar *which isn't clear.*

This says that Matt hates *unclear* grammar; perhaps Matt is a teacher who hates to read papers with poorly constructed sentences. The adjective clause is restrictive, or *essential*; it is needed to clarify what grammar Matt hates. In contrast, we have the nonrestrictive clause below:

> Matt hates grammar, *which isn't clear.*

This says that Matt hates grammar—period. Grammar is unclear. The adjective clause is not needed to clarify what grammar Matt hates; he hates *all* grammar. Hence the clause is called *nonrestrictive*, or *nonessential*. A nonrestrictive clause is set off from the main clause by commas in writing or by distinctive pauses in speech.

The following examples illustrate nonrestrictive adjective clauses. As these sentences suggest, such clauses are most natural and least disruptive when they modify a noun at the end of the main clause:

> My Aunt Mabel, *who belongs to the John Birch Society,* is always bothering us.
> We're always being bothered by my Aunt Mabel, *who belongs to the John Birch Society.*
> The millage, *which didn't seem likely to pass,* worried us considerably.
> We were worried about the millage, *which didn't seem likely to pass.*
> Cincinnati, *where Uncle Joe lives,* is Sally's favorite city.
> Sally's favorite city is Cincinnati, *where Uncle Joe lives.*

Nonrestrictive adjective clauses can usually be reduced if the introductory relative pronoun (usually *who* or *which*) is immediately followed by a form of the verb *to be.* We simply delete the relative pronoun and the form of *to be.* In many cases a reduced nonrestrictive

can be moved to the front of the sentence, the end of the sentence, or
both. Each of the examples below shows an adjectival construction
modifying a noun in subject position. The full nonrestrictive clause is
given first, followed by the reduced nonrestrictive in all the positions
supposedly possible. You might consider which position seems best in
each case, and why. Note that the full clause and its reductions are
always separated from the main clause by one or two commas, as needed:

> Ruth, *who was exhausted*, dragged herself up the stairs.
> Ruth, *exhausted*, dragged herself up the stairs.
> *Exhausted*, Ruth dragged herself up the stairs.
> Ruth dragged herself up the stairs, *exhausted*.

> Ms. Anderson, *who is our president*, will be in charge.
> *Our president*, Ms. Anderson, will be in charge.
> Ms. Anderson will be in charge, *our president*.

> Mindy, *who was whistling*, picked up her backpack.
> Mindy, *whistling*, picked up her backpack.
> *Whistling*, Mindy picked up her backpack.
> Mindy picked up her backpack, *whistling*.

> Rondi, *who was happy at last*, smiled.
> Rondi, *happy at last*, smiled.
> *Happy at last*, Rondi smiled.
> Rondi smiled, *happy at last*.

> Barber's grocery, *which is up ahead*, should have some.
> Barber's grocery, *up ahead*, should have some.
> *Up ahead*, Barber's grocery should have some.
> Barber's grocery should have some, *up ahead*.

> Colleen, *who was choking back the tears*, spoke calmly.
> Colleen, *choking back the tears*, spoke calmly.
> *Choking back the tears*, Colleen spoke calmly.
> Colleen spoke calmly, *choking back the tears*.

> Albert, *whose eyes were black with hate*, stared at her angrily.
> Albert, *(his) eyes black with hate*, stared at her angrily.
> *(His) eyes black with hate*, Albert stared at her angrily.
> Albert stared at her angrily, *(his) eyes black with hate*.

As these examples suggest, the reduced nonrestrictive clause occurs most
commonly and most comfortably in final or initial position.

A word about *sentence fragments* is again in order. Sometimes an
adjective clause is mispunctuated as if it were a complete T-unit:

> He dropped his briefcase. *Which he had just bought last week.*
> He admires Ayn Rand. *Whose books he has read over and over.*

To repair these sentence fragments, simply join them with a comma to the noun they modify:

> He dropped his briefcase, *which he had just bought last week.*
> He admires Ayn Rand, *whose books he has read over and over.*

Sometimes participial phrases are punctuated as sentence fragments. The first example below is headed by a present participle, *choking,* while the second is headed by a past participle, *exhausted:*

> Colleen spoke calmly. *Choking back the tears.*
> Ruth dragged herself up the stairs. *Exhausted from her day's work.*

Again, these can be repaired by joining them to the main clause:

> Colleen spoke calmly, *choking back the tears.*
> Ruth dragged herself up the stairs, *exhausted from her day's work.*

Note, however, that a sentence fragment can occasionally be used quite effectively:

> Ruth dragged herself up the stairs. She was tired. *Exhausted.*

By punctuating *exhausted* as a separate sentence, we can emphasize Ruth's extreme fatigue. Just as the run-on sentence can sometimes be effective, so can the sentence fragment.

Another problem with participles, however, is that we may not be able to tell what they modify. Such ambiguous constructions are called *dangling participles:*

> Alvin can reach it better than Mary, *standing on the ladder.*

Here it's not entirely clear who is standing on the ladder. An adjectival modifier is usually taken to describe the nearest noun, which in this case is *Mary.* But in this particular sentence, logic suggests that it's Alvin who is on the ladder. Usually it helps to move the participial phrase next to the noun modified:

> Alvin, *standing on the ladder,* can reach it better than Mary.

Another solution is to change the participial phrase to an adverb clause:

> Alvin can reach it better than Mary, *because he is standing on the ladder.*

A slightly different kind of dangling participle is illustrated below.

> *Standing on the corner,* trains rush by every hour.

Here, the problem is that the subject of the main clause is not the same as the subject of the sentence underlying the participial phrase. More specifically, the sentence doesn't tell us who is standing on the corner (surely it's not the trains). The main clause should tell us who is doing the standing:

> *Standing on the corner,* you can see trains rush by every hour.

Summary

There are two major types of dependent clauses that may be added to describe or "modify" the entire main clause or some part of it. The *adverb clause* usually describes the action indicated in the main clause. The *adjective clause* describes some noun in the main clause. The punctuation conventions are as follows:

1. *Adverb clause and its reductions.*
    a. If an adverb clause (or its reduction) occurs before a main clause, it is followed by a comma:

    > *If it's snowing,* we won't leave.

    b. If an adverb clause (or its reduction) occurs after a main clause, it is often preceded by a comma, but not always:

    > We won't leave, *if it's snowing;* or
    > We won't leave *if it's snowing.*

    c. An adverb clause rarely interrupts the main clause but, when it does, it is set off by commas:

    > The truth, *if you want to know,* is that he's lazy.   ｡

2. *Adjective clause and its reductions.*
    a. One type of adjective clause is called *restrictive,* meaning that it is essential for clarification.

    > Matt hates grammar *which isn't clear.* (This means, "Matt hates unclear grammar.")

    The essential adjective clause or its reduction is never separated from the main clause by a comma.

    b. The other type of adjective clause is called nonrestrictive, meaning that it is nonessential for clarification:

    > Matt hates grammar, *which isn't clear.* (This means, "Matt hates all grammar; grammar isn't clear.")

    The nonessential adjective clause or its reduction is always separated from the main clause by one or two commas, as needed:

    > Colleen, *who was choking back the tears,* spoke calmly.
    > Colleen, *choking back the tears,* spoke calmly.
    > *Choking back the tears,* Colleen spoke calmly.
    > Colleen spoke calmly, *choking back the tears.*

Notes

1. In the case of writing, nonverbal communication would include torn paper, ink smudges, and typographical errors—in short, all those things which communicate writers' attitudes toward their subject and/or their audience.

2. This hypothetical sequence is based partly on my own observations, but mainly on my inferences from Klima and Bellugi-Klima 1966; Dale 1976, p. 107; Cazden 1972, p. 54; and Brown 1973, p. 274.

3. The young child seems to consider irregular past tense forms as one unit or morpheme (the indissoluble word *ate*) rather than as two (the verb *eat*, plus the concept *past*). When children first learn the regular rule for forming past tenses, they overgeneralize the rule, producing such forms as *eated*, *goed*, *buyed* and so forth. Some children overgeneralize the rule by adding the regular past tense ending to the irregular past form, producing such forms as *ated*, *wented*, and *boughted* (and of course the child may treat some verbs one way and other verbs the other way). Only when children stop producing such overgeneralizations can they be said to recognize that forms such as *ate* convey two separable concepts, in this case the concept of eating and the concept of pastness.

4. At first, *did* seems to be a single unit for the child, similar to *ate*. In questions and negatives, forms of the *do* verb ordinarily are grammatical markers only; they convey no independent meaning. Hence no morpheme is added in this step.

5. Word order makes it clear that *me* expresses the agent, so in context the change from *me* to *I* is a matter of form rather than of meaning. Still, the change from *me* to *I* in subject position may occur early in the developmental sequence—assuming that the child initially used *me* as an all-purpose first person singular pronoun. Some children, of course, adopt a different form as an all-purpose first person singular (my own son used *my* in all positions). Other children may differentiate the three forms from the very outset.

6. Indeed, as I was in the very process of writing this, my six-year-old son (always a rich source of examples) handed me a jumble of letters he had just typed. I smiled in absent-minded appreciation and tried to return the paper to him, but he persisted with the question "What does it say?" I looked again, this time expecting to find meaning, and I immediately found the word hidden amongst the numbers in his last line of type: 1½o½v½e. An atypical example, of course. But it illustrates the basic nature of proficient listening and reading: they involve an active search for meaning.

7. This tendency is also illustrated by an amusing anecdote about my son John, who at the time was just out of kindergarten. When I returned from

trying to locate John's missing friend Charlie, I found taped to the screen door a note which said, simply but eloquently:

MOM
JOHN

Given the situational context, it was clear that John had gone looking for Charlie too. However, the *real* message seems to have been something like: "I'm writing you this note because I know I'm not supposed to leave our yard without telling you." Thus the minimal message reflects the child's underlying propositions.

8. In many cases such omission may merely reflect the child's spoken dialect. For example, many speakers of black English frequently omit such endings in their speech; indeed, they may even omit such endings when reading aloud from a "standard" text—see pp. 31-32. Teachers need to understand the structure of their students' dialects in order to work with them most effectively.

9. At an even earlier stage, prewriters may think they have expressed meaning in written symbols (writing), but that only someone else can tell what that meaning is—hence the title of Clay's 1975 book *What Did I Write?*

10. Here is the full passage:

The crackle of the rifle volley cut the suddenly still air. It appeared to go on, as a solid volley, for perhaps a full minute or a little longer.

Some of the students dived to the ground, crawling on the grass in terror. Others stood shocked or half crouched, apparently believing the troops were firing into the air. Some of the rifle barrels were pointed upward.

Near the top of the hill at the corner of Taylor Hall, a student crumpled over, spun sideways and fell to the ground, shot in the head.

When the firing stopped, a slim girl, wearing a cowboy shirt and faded jeans, was lying face down on the road at the edge of the parking lot, blood pouring out onto the macadam, about 10 feet from this reporter.

11. The answers are: (1) aren't (2) Most (3) three (4) and (5) 40 (6) of (7) most (8) is (9) as (10) Beavers (11) dams (12) They (13) paws (14) their (15) tree (16) pointed (17) beaver (18) tree (19) about.

12. At an earlier stage, prewriters are often convinced that they have written *something* meaningful, but that only someone else can figure out what they have said (Clay 1975).

13. Thanks to the efforts of the Michigan Council of Teachers of English, the state writing objectives have recently been revised to reflect a much more realistic view of children's writing.

14. They also may be sacrificing syntactic maturity for increased "correctness." See Mellon 1976.

15. "If we can convince our students that spelling, punctuation, and usage are less important than content, we have removed a major obstacle in their developing the ability to write." ("Students' Right to Their Own Language," *College Composition and Communication* 25 [1974]: 8.)

16. "Secretary's Reports," *College Composition and Communication* 25 (1974): 339.

17. In the long run, however, argumentative writing seems to foster (or at

least call forth) the greatest degree of syntactic complexity, and expository writing ranks second (Pope 1974; Kantor and Perron 1977).

18.   Exercises 2-4 are taken from the *Communicating* series by Botel and Dawkins (1973). Exercise 2 is from Book 3, pp. 199-200, "Another Way to Add Sentences"; Exercise 3 is from Book 6, pp. 32-33; Exercise 4 is from Book 6, pp. 117-118, "The Absolute Construction."

19.   From Mill's Inaugural Address at the University of St. Andrews, 1867. In Francis W. Garforth, ed., *John Stuart Mill on Education* (New York: Teachers College Press, 1971): pp. 174-175.

20.   This is not the place to argue the merits of traditional school grammars or of teaching grammar in general, but three points might be briefly noted: the definitions and terms are often unclear and/or complex (for one reason or another, this is true of most grammars); the prescriptive rules of traditional school grammars are often not relevant, either because they are based upon a different language structure (Latin) or because they ignore the current usage of the educated; and last, there is considerable evidence that the formal teaching of grammar (traditional or otherwise) has, in and of itself, little effect upon usage or upon the communicative processes of listening, speaking, reading, and writing (see pp. 3-6 and 88-89). For evidence to support the latter point, see the *Encyclopedia of Educational Research*, 1950, pp. 392-393; 1960, pp. 459-463; 1969, pp. 451-453.

21.   The prepositional phrase is an exception to this definition, since the preposition is not usually considered a head word, modified by its following nominal.

22.   The following list reveals another problem with the term "indefinite pronoun": that not all of the so-called indefinite pronouns are actually indefinite.

23.   The ordinal numbers (*first*, *second*, *third*, etc.) form a different kind of category. Unlike the cardinal determiners, the ordinal determiners must be preceded by an article, a demonstrative, or a possessive: You don't get a *second* chance, versus, You get *two* chances.

24.   The modals *can*, *shall*, *will*, *may*, and *must* are considered to be present tense forms. For historical reasons, the other modals are considered to be past tense forms.

25.   In the first example, it is the possessive form of the noun that modifies a following noun. When the base form of the noun modifies a following noun (as in the second and third examples), it is called a *noun adjunct*.

26.   A noun or noun phrase modifying a preceding noun is traditionally called an *appositive*. The appositive is said to be "in apposition with" the noun modified. Ordinarily, an appositive is both preceded by a comma and followed by a comma (unless it occurs at the end of the sentence).

27.   An adjectivally-functioning absolute is basically a clause with a *be* verb missing: *his eyes [were] black with hate.*

28.   As this awkward sentence might suggest, the superlative of adverbs is rarely used.

29.   When we look at adverbs of time (below), it is even more obvious that adverbs can modify entire clauses: We cleaned the garage *yesterday*; *yesterday* we cleaned the garage. In these sentences it seems clear that the adverb *yesterday* modifies the entire action and not some particular word.

30.   The category *adverb* also includes intensifiers like *especially, extraordinarily, really, too,* and *very*. But since intensifiers are a relatively minor subcategory, we will omit them from further discussion.

31.   Adverbial clauses of time are often reducible if they contain present participles: He soaked his toupee *while (he was) shaving.* Thus we might include present participle phrases as a separate category. The decision not to do so is admittedly arbitrary.

32.   The most common kind of adverbially-functioning absolute is structured like a clause, except that it has the word *being* instead of a present or past tense *be* form: Dinner *being* almost over... (absolute), versus, Dinner *was* almost over (clause). This kind of absolute usually serves as an adverbial of reason. Since adverbially-functioning absolutes are relatively rare in modern English, they will receive no further discussion.

33.   This is the same as the T-unit, as Kellogg Hunt has defined it. See pp. 68-69 here, and see his article "Recent Measures in Syntactic Development." *Elementary English* 43 (Nov. 1966): 732-739.

34.   Conjunctive adverbs are sometimes called transitional adverbs, adverbial connectors, sentence adverbials, or simply sentence connectors.

35.   For brevity, we have omitted the pairs of coordinators that are called *correlative conjunctions*. The major pairs are *either/or*, and *neither/nor*.

36.   In his *Modern English Usage*, Fowler suggests using only *that* to introduce restrictive clauses, and reserving *which* and *who* for nonrestrictive clauses (1965, p. 626). However, he admits that this practice is not common, even among the "best" writers.

References

Applebee, Arthur N. "ERIC/RCS Report—Writing across the Curriculum: The London Projects." *English Journal* 66 (Dec. 1977): 81-85.

Baldwin, James. *Nobody Knows My Name.* New York: Dial Press, 1961.

Bateman, Donald, and Zidonis, Frank. *The Effect of a Study of Transformational Grammar on the Writing of Ninth and Tenth Graders.* Research Report No. 6. Urbana, Ill.: National Council of Teachers of English, 1966.

Beers, James W., and Henderson, Edmund H. "A Study of Developing Orthographic Concepts among First Graders." *Research in the Teaching of English* 12 (1977): 133-48.

Bellugi-Klima, Ursula. "Simplification in Children's Language." In *Language Acquisition: Models and Methods,* edited by R. Huxley and E. Ingram, pp. 95-119. New York: Academic Press, 1971.

Bloomfield, Leonard. *Language.* New York: Holt, Rinehart & Winston, 1933.

Bormuth, John R. "The Cloze Readability Procedure." *Elementary English* 45 (1968): 429-36. Reprinted in *Readability in 1968,* edited by John Bormuth, pp. 40-47. Urbana, Ill.: National Council of Teachers of English, 1968.

————. "Literacy in the Classroom." In *Help for the Reading Teacher: New Directions in Research,* edited by William D. Page, pp. 60-90. Urbana, Ill.: National Conference on Research in English, 1975.

Botel, Morton, and Dawkins, John. *Communicating: The Heath English Series.* Indianapolis, Ind.: D.C. Heath & Co., 1973.

Braddock, Richard; Lloyd-Jones, Richard; and Schoer, Lowell. *Research in Written Composition.* Urbana, Ill.: National Council of Teachers of English, 1963.

Britton, James N. "Now That You Go to School." In *Children and Writing in the Elementary School,* edited by Richard L. Larson, pp. 3-17. New York: Oxford University Press, 1975. Reprinted from Britton's *Language and Learning.* Penguin Press, 1970; Pelican Books, 1972, pp. 164-70, 173-180.

Brown, Roger. *A First Language: The Early Stages.* Cambridge, Mass.: Harvard University Press, 1973.

Brown, Roger, and Bellugi-Klima, Ursula. "Three Processes in the Child's Acquisition of Syntax." *Harvard Educational Review* 34 (1964): 133-51.

Brown, Roger, and Fraser, Colin. "The Acquisition of Syntax." In *Verbal Behavior and Learning: Problems and Processes,* edited by Charles N. Cofer and Barbara Musgrave, pp. 158-201. New York: McGraw-Hill, 1963.

Burke, Carolyn. "Preparing Elementary Teachers to Teach Reading." In *Miscue Analysis: Applications to Reading Instruction,* edited by Kenneth S. Goodman, pp. 15-29. Urbana, Ill.: ERIC Clearinghouse on Reading and Communication Skills and the National Council of Teachers of English, 1973.

159

Burling, Robbins. *English in Black and White*. New York: Holt, Rinehart & Winston, 1973.

Calvert, Kenneth H. "K-Ratio Index." 1971. Available from the Educational Resources Information Center: ED 091 722.

Carton, Aaron S. *Orientation to Reading*. Rowley, Mass.: Newbury House Publishers, 1976.

Cazden, Courtney B. *Child Language and Education*. New York: Holt, Rinehart & Winston, 1972.

Chaika, Elaine. "Grammars and Teaching." *College English* 39 (1978): 770-83.

Chase, Stuart. *The Power of Words*. New York: Harcourt Brace Jovanovich, 1954.

Chatman, Seymour B. "Linguistics and Teaching Introductory Literature." *Language Learning* 7 (1956-57): 3-10.

Chomsky, Carol. *The Acquisition of Syntax in Children from 5 to 10*. Cambridge, Mass.: M.I.T. Press, 1969.

Chomsky, Noam. *Language and Mind*. New York: Harcourt Brace Jovanovich, 1968.

Christensen, Francis. *The Christensen Rhetoric Program: The Sentence and the Paragraph*. New York: Harper & Row, 1968a.

———. *Notes toward a New Rhetoric*. New York: Harper & Row, 1967.

———. "The Problem of Defining a Mature Style." *English Journal* 57 (April 1968b): 572-79.

Christensen, Francis, and Christensen, Bonniejean. *A New Rhetoric*. New York: Harper & Row, 1976.

Clark, Herbert H., and Clark, Eve V. *Psychology and Language: An Introduction to Psycholinguistics*. New York: Harcourt Brace Jovanovich, 1977.

Clay, Marie M. *What Did I Write?* Auckland, New Zealand: Heinemann Educational Books, 1975.

Conference on College Composition and Communication. "Secretary's Reports." *College Composition and Communication* 25 (1974): 327-40.

———. *Students' Right to Their Own Language*. Urbana, Ill.: National Council of Teachers of English, 1974.

Cooper, Charles R. "An Outline for Writing Sentence-Combining Problems." *English Journal* 62 (Jan. 1973): 96-102, 108.

Cooper, Charles R., and Odell, Lee, eds. *Evaluating Writing: Describing, Measuring, Judging*. Urbana, Ill.: National Council of Teachers of English, 1977.

Cooper, Charles R., and Petrosky, Anthony R. "A Psycholinguistic View of the Fluent Reading Process." *Journal of Reading* 20 (1976): 184-207.

Cooperative Sequential Tests of Educational Progress (STEP): Writing. Princeton, N.J.: Educational Testing Service, 1957.

Culhane, Joseph. "Cloze Procedures and Comprehension." *The Reading Teacher* 23 (1970): 410-13, 464.

Cummings, E. E. *Collected Poems*. New York: Harcourt Brace Jovanovich, 1963. Poem 13.

Dale, Philip S. *Language Development: Structure and Function*. 2nd ed. New York: Holt, Rinehart & Winston, 1976.

DeBoer, John J. "Grammar in Language Teaching." *Elementary English* 36 (1959): 413-21.

Diederich, Paul B. *Measuring Growth in English*. Urbana, Ill.: National Council of Teachers of English, 1974.

Ebbitt, Wilma R., and Ebbitt, David R. *Index to English*. 6th ed. Glenview, Ill.: Scott, Foresman & Company, 1977.

Educational Testing Service. "Multiple-Choice Test Assesses Writing Ability." *Findings* 4 (no. 1, 1977): 1-4.

Elley, W. B.; Barham, J. H.; Lamb, H.; and Wyllie, M. "The Role of Grammar in a Secondary School English Curriculum." *Research in the Teaching of English* 10 (1976): 5-21. Reprinted from *New Zealand Journal of Educational Studies* 10 (May 1975): 26-42.

Ellison, Ralph. *Invisible Man*. New York: Random House, 1952.

Emig, Janet. *The Composing Processes of Twelfth Graders*. Research Report No. 13. Urbana, Ill.: National Council of Teachers of English, 1971.

Encyclopedia of Educational Research, ed. Walter S. Monroe. Rev. ed. New York: Macmillan Co., 1950.

Encyclopedia of Educational Research, ed. Chester W. Harris. 3rd ed. New York: Macmillan Co., 1960.

Erskine, John. "A Note on the Writer's Craft." In *Twentieth Century English*, edited by William Skinkle Knickerbocker. New York: Philosophical Library, 1946.

Fagan, William T.; Cooper, Charles R.; and Jensen, Julie M. *Measures for Research and Evaluation in the English Language Arts*. Urbana, Ill.: ERIC Clearinghouse on Reading and Communication Skills and the National Council of Teachers of English, 1975.

Farrell, Edmund J. *Deciding the Future: A Forecast of Responsibilities of Secondary Teachers of English, 1970-2000 AD*. Research Report No. 12. Urbana, Ill.: National Council of Teachers of English, 1971.

Fowler, H. W. *A Dictionary of Modern English Usage*. 2nd rev. ed. London: Oxford University Press, 1965.

Fries, Charles Carpenter. *The Structure of English: An Introduction to the Construction of English Sentences*. New York: Harcourt Brace Jovanovich, 1952.

Gebhardt, Richard. "Imagination and Discipline in the Writing Class." *English Journal* 66 (Dec. 1977): 26-32.

————. "The Timely Teetertotter: Balancing Discipline and Creativity in Writing Classes." *Language Arts* 54 (1977): 673-78.

Gere, Anne Ruggles. "Writing and WRITING." *English Journal* 66 (Nov. 1977): 60-64.

Gibson, Walker. *Persona: A Style Study for Readers and Writers*. New York: Random House, 1969.

Gliserman, Martin. "An Act of Theft: Teaching Grammar." *College English* 39 (1978): 791-800.

Goodman, Kenneth S. "A Linguistic Study of Cues and Miscues in Reading." *Elementary English* 42 (1965): 639-43.

Goodman, Kenneth S., and Buck, Catherine. "Dialect Barriers to Reading Comprehension Revisited." *The Reading Teacher* 27 (1973): 6-13.

Goodman, Kenneth S., and Burke, Carolyn L. *Theoretically Based Studies of Patterns of Miscues in Oral Reading Performance*. Detroit: Wayne State University Press, 1973. Available from the Educational Resources Information Center: ED 079 708.

Goodman, Yetta M. "Developing Reading Proficiency." In *Findings of Research in Miscue Analysis: Classroom Implications*, edited by P. David Allen and Dorothy J. Watson, pp. 113-28. Urbana, Ill.: Clearinghouse on Reading and Communication Skills and the National Council of Teachers of English, 1976.

Goodman, Yetta, and Burke, Carolyn L. *Reading Miscue Inventory Manual*. New York: Macmillan Co., 1972.

Gould, Victor E. *Experiments in Effective Writing*. New York: Harcourt Brace Jovanovich, 1972.

Graves, Donald H. "Let's Get Rid of the Welfare Mess in the Teaching of Writing." *Language Arts* 53 (1976): 645-51.

Grimm Brothers, *Grimms' Fairy Tales*. Translated by E. V. Lucas, Lucy Crane, and Marian Edwardes. New York: Grosset & Dunlap, 1945.

Grommon, Alfred H., ed. *Reviews of Selected Published Tests in English*. Urbana, Ill.: National Council of Teachers of English, 1976.

Hughes, Theone O. "Sentence Combining: A Means of Increasing Reading Comprehension." Kalamazoo, Mich.: Western Michigan University, 1975. Available from the Educational Resources Information Center: ED 112 421.

Hunt, Barbara Carey. "Black Dialect and Third and Fourth Graders' Performance on the Gray Oral Reading Test." *Reading Research Quarterly* 10 (1974-75): 103-23.

Hunt, Kellogg W. "Early Blooming and Late Blooming Syntactic Structures." In *Evaluating Writing: Describing, Measuring, Judging*, edited by Charles R. Cooper and Lee Odell, pp. 91-104. Urbana, Ill.: National Council of Teachers of English, 1977.

_____. *Grammatical Structures Written at Three Grade Levels*. Research Report No. 3. Urbana, Ill.: National Council of Teachers of English, 1965.

_____. "Recent Measures in Syntactic Development." *Elementary English* 43 (1966): 732-39.

_____. *Syntactic Maturity in Schoolchildren and Adults*. Monographs of the Society for Research in Child Development, No. 134. Chicago: University of Chicago Press, 1970.

Jacobs, Roderick A., and Rosenbaum, Peter S. *Transformations, Style, and Meaning*. Waltham, Mass.: Xerox College Publishing, 1971.

Jespersen, Otto. *Essentials of English Grammar*. 1933. Reprint. University, Ala.: University of Alabama Press, 1964.

_____. *Language: Its Nature, Development and Origin*. London: George Allen and Unwin, 1922.

Johnson, Terry D. "Language Experience: We Can't All Write What We Can Say." *The Reading Teacher* 31 (1977): 297-99.

Kantor, Ken, and Perron, Jack. "Thinking and Writing: Creativity in the Modes of Discourse." *Language Arts* 54 (1977): 742-49.

Katz, Sharon. "Linguistics and the Study of Shakespearean Plays." In *Teaching English Linguistically: Five Experimental Curricula*, edited by Harvey Minkoff, pp. 113-78. New Rochelle, N.Y.: Iona College Press, 1971.

Kimball, J. P. "Seven Principles of Surface Structure Parsing in Natural Language." *Cognition* 2 (1973): 15-47.

Klarner, Walter E.; Williams, James M.; and Harp, Harold L. *Writing by Design*. Boston: Houghton Mifflin Co., 1977.

Klima, E. S., and Bellugi-Klima, Ursula. "Syntactic Regularities in the Speech of Children." In *Psycholinguistic Papers*, edited by J. Lyons and R. J. Wales, pp. 183-208. Edinburgh: Edinburgh University Press, 1966.

Koch, Kenneth. *Wishes, Lies, and Dreams*. New York: Random House, 1970.

Larson, Richard L., ed. *Children and Writing in the Elementary School*. New York: Oxford University Press, 1975.

Lester, Mark. *Words and Sentences*. New York: Random House, 1973.

Levin, Harry, and Kaplan, Eleanor L. "Grammatical Structure and Reading." In *Basic Studies on Reading*, edited by Harry Levin and Joanna P. Williams, pp. 119-33. New York: Basic Books, 1970.

Loban, Walter D. *Language Development: Kindergarten through Grade Twelve*. Research Report No. 18. Urbana, Ill.: National Council of Teachers of English, 1976.

―――. *The Language of Elementary School Children*. Research Report No. 1. Urbana, Ill.: National Council of Teachers of English, 1963.

―――. "The Limitless Possibilities for Increasing Knowledge about Language." *Elementary English* 47 (1970): 624-30.

Lundsteen, Sara W., ed. *Help for the Teacher of Written Composition: New Directions in Research*. Urbana, Ill.: National Conference on Research in English, 1976.

MacKay, David M.; Thompson, Brian; and Schaub, Pamela. *Breakthrough to Literacy (Teacher's Manual): The Theory and Practice of Teaching Initial Reading and Writing*. Schools Council Programme in Linguistics and English Teaching. Glendale, Calif.: Bowmar, 1970.

Malmstrom, Jean. *Grammar Basics: A Reading/Writing Approach*. Rochelle Park, N.J.: Hayden Book Co., 1977. First edition (1968) was titled *An Introduction to Modern Grammar*.

Malmstrom, Jean, and Weaver, Constance. *Transgrammar: English Structure, Style, and Dialects*. Glenview, Ill.: Scott, Foresman & Co., 1973.

Martin, Bill, Jr., and Brogan, Peggy. *Sounds of a Powwow*. Holt, Rinehart & Winston, 1974.

―――. *Teaching Suggestions for 'Sounds Jubilee' and 'Sounds Freedomring.'* New York: Holt, Rinehart & Winston, 1975.

Martin, Nancy, and Mulford, Jeremy. "Spelling, etc." In *Children and Writing in the Elementary School*, edited by Richard L. Larson, pp. 375-95. New York: Oxford University Press, 1975. Reprinted from *Children Using Language*, edited by Anthony Jones and Jeremy Mulford, pp. 153-73. London: Oxford University Press, 1971.

McCaig, Roger A. "What Research and Evaluation Tell Us about Teaching Written Expression in the Elementary School." In *The Language Arts Teacher in Action*, edited by Constance Weaver and Rollin Douma, pp. 46-56. Kalamazoo, Mich.: Western Michigan University, 1977a. Available from National Council of Teachers of English.

―――. "What Your Director of Instruction Needs to Know about Standardized English Tests." *Language Arts* 54 (1977b): 491-95.

————. *The Writing of Elementary School Children: A Model for Evaluation.* Grosse Pointe, Mich.: Grosse Pointe Public School System, 1972.

Mellon, John C. *National Assessment and the Teaching of English.* Urbana, Ill.: National Council of Teachers of English, 1975.

————. "Round Two of the National Writing Assessment—Interpreting the Apparent Decline of Writing Ability: A Review." *Research in the Teaching of English* 10 (1976): 66-74.

————. *Transformational Sentence-Combining.* Research Report No. 10. Urbana, Ill.: National Council of Teachers of English, 1969.

Michigan Department of Education. *Minimal Performance Objectives for Communication Skills Education in Michigan.* Lansing, Mich., 1971.

Mill, John Stuart. *John Stuart Mill on Education,* edited by Francis W. Garforth. New York: Teachers College Press, 1971.

Minkoff, Harvey, and Katz, Sharon. "Spoken and Written English: Teaching Passive Grammar." *College Composition and Communication* 24 (1973): 157-62.

National Assessment of Educational Progress. *Writing Mechanics, 1969-1974: A Capsule Description of Changes in Writing Mechanics.* Report No. 05-W-01. Denver, Colorado: National Assessment of Educational Progress, 1975.

"NCTE Criticizes Standardized Tests." *English Journal* 64 (Feb. 1975): 30.

"NCTE's Position on Dialect." *English Journal* 64 (Feb. 1975): 28-29.

Ney, James W. "Notes towards a Psycholinguistic Model of the Writing Process." *Research in the Teaching of English* 8 (1974): 157-69.

O'Donnell, Roy C. "A Test of Perception of Syntactic Alternatives." 1973. Available from the Educational Resources Information Center: ED 077 025.

O'Donnell, Roy C.; Griffin, William J.; and Norris, Raymond C. *Syntax of Kindergarten and Elementary School Children: A Transformational Analysis.* Research Report No. 8. Urbana, Ill.: National Council of Teachers of English, 1967.

O'Donnell, Roy C., and Smith, William L. "Increasing Ninth-Grade Students' Awareness of Syntactic Structures through Direct Instruction." *Research in the Teaching of English* 9 (1975): 257-62.

O'Hare, Frank. *Sentence Combining: Improving Student Writing without Formal Grammar Instruction.* Research Report No. 15. Urbana, Ill.: National Council of Teachers of English, 1973.

————. *Sentencecraft.* Lexington, Mass.: Ginn & Co., 1975.

Perron, Jack. "Beginning Writing: It's All in the Mind." *Language Arts* 53 (1976): 652-57.

Petrosky, Anthony R. "Grammar Instruction: What We Know." *English Journal* 66 (Dec. 1977): 86-88.

Pollack, Irwin, and Pickett, J. M. "Intelligibility of Excerpts from Fluent Speech: Auditory vs. Structural Context." *Journal of Verbal Learning and Verbal Behavior* 3 (1964): 79-84.

Pope, Mike. "The Syntax of Fourth Graders' Narrative and Explanatory Speech." *Research in the Teaching of English* 8 (1974): 219-27.

Porter, William S. *The Complete Works of O. Henry.* Garden City, New York: Doubleday, Doran & Co., 1936.

Postman, Neil, and Weingartner, Charles. *Linguistics: A Revolution in Teaching.* New York: Dell Publishing Co., 1966.

Read, Charles. *Children's Categorization of Speech Sounds in English.* Research Report No. 17. Urbana, Ill.: National Council of Teachers of English, 1975.

Roberts, Paul. *Patterns of English.* New York: Harcourt Brace Jovanovich, 1956.

Rutherford, William E. *Sentence Sense.* New York: Harcourt Brace Jovanovich, 1973.

Shaughnessy, Mina P. *Errors and Expectations: A Guide for the Teacher of Basic Writing.* New York: Oxford University Press, 1977.

Simons, Herbert D., and Johnson, Kenneth R. "Black English Syntax and Reading Interference." *Research in the Teaching of English* 8 (1974): 339-58.

SLATE Steering Committee. "Back to the Basics." SLATE Starter Sheets, Vol. 1. Urbana, Ill.: National Council of Teachers of English, 1976.

———. "Standardized Testing." SLATE Starter Sheets, Vol. 2. Urbana, Ill.: National Council of Teachers of English, 1977.

Slobin, Dan I., and Welsh, Charles A. "Elicited Imitation as a Research Tool in Developmental Psycholinguistics." In *Studies of Child Language Development,* edited by Charles A. Ferguson and Dan Isaac Slobin, pp. 485-97. New York: Holt, Rinehart & Winston, 1973.

Smith, Frank. *Comprehension and Learning: A Conceptual Framework for Teachers.* New York: Holt, Rinehart & Winston, 1975.

———. *Psycholinguistics and Reading.* New York: Holt, Rinehart & Winston, 1973.

———. *Understanding Reading.* 2nd ed. New York: Holt, Rinehart & Winston, 1978.

Stauffer, Russell G., and Cramer, Ronald. *Teaching Critical Reading at the Primary Level.* Newark, Del.: International Reading Association, 1968.

Strohner, Hans, and Nelson, Keith E. "The Young Child's Development of Sentence Comprehension: Influence of Event Probability, Nonverbal Context, Syntactic Form, and Strategies." *Child Development* 45 (1974): 567-76.

Strong, William. *Sentence Combining.* New York: Random House, 1973.

———. "Sentence-Combining: Back to Basics and Beyond." *English Journal* 65 (Feb. 1976): 56, 60-64.

Sutton, Gary A. "Do We Need to Teach a Grammar Terminology?" *English Journal* 65 (Dec. 1976): 37-40.

Warren, Richard M., and Warren, Roslyn P. "Auditory Illusions and Confusions." *Scientific American* 223 (1970): 30-36.

Warriner, John E., and Griffith, Francis. *English Grammar and Composition Series.* Heritage ed. New York: Harcourt Brace Jovanovich, 1977.

Weaver, Constance. "How Do We Read? A Primer for Teachers." Preliminary materials. Kalamazoo, Mich.: Western Michigan University, 1976.

———. *Psycholinguistics and Reading: From Process to Practice* (tentative title). Cambridge, Mass.: Winthrop Publishers, forthcoming.

———. "Using Context: Before or After?" *Language Arts* 54 (1977), 880-86.

Weber, Rose-Marie. "First-Graders' Use of Grammatical Context in Reading." In *Basic Studies on Reading,* edited by Harry Levin and Joanna P. Williams, pp. 147-63. New York: Basic Books, 1970.

Author

Constance Weaver received a Ph.D. in English from Michigan State University and is presently an Associate Professor of English at Western Michigan University. She specializes in applied linguistics and English education, and is the author of articles and books on grammar, dialects, reading, and the language arts.